T0038791

"Dispensing his vast linguistic expertise with the lightest and deftest of touches, John McWhorter shows brilliantly how the 'nastiest' words can teach us about the dynamic and unruly nature of all language. Anyone interested in words (and not just the nasty ones) should read this book."

—Joe Moran, author of *First You Write a Sentence*

"*Nine Nasty Words* takes the reader round the back of the English language, only to show—with irrepressible humor and a dash of forbearance—how what we find there is central to who we are."

—Rebecca Gowers, author of
Horrible Words: A Guide to the Misuse of English

"If you want to get down and dirty in the gutter of English (and, be honest, who doesn't?) you'd better go with a guide who knows his sh*t. McWhorter gives a jovial, expert tour of the 'bedrock swears,' from the offensive and profane to the merely 'salty,' not just where they came from, but how they have shifted and morphed in force, meaning, grammar and in the effect they produce."

—Arika Okrent, author of *In the Land of Invented Languages*

"Only a kick-ass writer could wrest such erudite historical fun from language's sh*thouse. Damn, this is one hell of a book, and this p***y will never curse the same again."

—Ann Patty, author of *Living with a Dead Language*

NINE
NASTY
W*RDS

NINE
NASTY
W*RDS

English in the Gutter: Then, Now, and Forever

JOHN McWHORTER

AVERY

an imprint of Penguin Random House

New York

AVERY

an imprint of Penguin Random House LLC
penguinrandomhouse.com

Most Avery books are available at special quantity discounts for bulk purchase
for sales promotions, premiums, fund-raising, and educational needs.
Special books or book excerpts also can be created to fit specific needs.
For details, write SpecialMarkets@penguinrandomhouse.com.

Library of Congress Cataloging-in-Publication Data

Names: McWhorter, John H., author.
Title: Nine nasty words: English in the gutter:
then, now, and forever / by John McWhorter.
Description: [New York]: Avery, [2021]
Identifiers: LCCN 2020030508 (print) | LCCN 2020030509 (ebook) |
ISBN 9780593188798 (hardcover) | ISBN 9780593188804 (ebook)
Subjects: LCSH: English language—Obscene words.
Classification: LCC PE3724.O3 M38 2021 (print) |
LCC PE3724.O3 (ebook) | DDC 179/.5—dc23
LC record available at https://lccn.loc.gov/2020030508
LC ebook record available at https://lccn.loc.gov/2020030509
p.   cm.

ISBN (paperback) 9780593421383

Printed in the United States of America
1st Printing

Book design by Laura K. Corless

For Vanessa Hamilton McWhorter,
who I get the feeling is going to have a witty feel for
at least some of these words as we travel on

CONTENTS

INTRODUCTION

Babe Ruth's parents had a rocky marriage. Mr. Ruth ran a bar. Apparently the bartender and Mrs. Ruth had eyes for each other and did something about it. Mr. Ruth knew it and got a lawyer to have the bartender sign an affidavit. The document survives, and reads:

> *I the under sign fucked Mrs Geo. H, Ruth March 12 1906 on her dinging room floor whitch She ask me to do*

That piece of paper is what many of us would find the most interesting thing concerning Babe Ruth until he broke baseball's home run record in 1920, despite that he was neither the miscreant nor the cuckold involved. Why?

A friend of mine's mother had a certain fondness for "blue" language and, as her children became teenagers, began cursing rather freely in their presence. One Christmas Day, when everything seemed to be going wrong and she was complaining about it, her daughter said, "Mom, I thought on Christmas everybody was supposed to be jolly!" The mother shot back, "Oh, jolly shit!" My friend was still laughing at that years later, when it cracked me up, too, and I cherish the memory of that episode forty years after it happened—despite that I wasn't even there. Why?

And you're probably waiting for me to get to George Carlin's famous routine about the "Seven Words You Can Never Say on Television." It would be downright antisocial not to list them now: *shit*, *piss*, *fuck*, *cunt*, *cocksucker*, *motherfucker*, and *tits*. The question is, though, why that routine is so well remembered almost fifty years later, while some of us would be hard-pressed to remember anything else Carlin said, or anything that comedian David Brenner, also a phenom at the time, ever said at all—and if you draw a blank on Brenner completely, case in point.

———

The Babe Ruth tale entices because we are intrigued to see people in a post-Victorian era, when public mores were so much starchier, using a word we even today think of as distinctly dirty. Perhaps nothing could make long-gone people seem realer to us than evidence that they used words like *fuck*. Profanity channels our essence.

"Oh, jolly shit!" is funny first in that a woman—a mother, no less—was saying something with such a smutty feel in front of her kids but also in that it shows how our urge to curse often bypasses our fundamental instinct to make sense. What did "Oh, jolly shit!" *mean*, and if the answer is nothing, then why do we say such things? "What the fuck is that?" is subject to similar questions—what part of speech, exactly, is *fuck* in that sentence? Profanity channels our essence without always making sense.

And Carlin's routine still resonates in pointing out the wholly arbitrary power of curse words. Carlin coolly rattled them off in a way that no comedian could have on a commercially released album ten years before, and the sky did not fall in. But even in recent years, then–Vice President Joe Biden made national news by not saying but whispering, "This is a big fucking deal!" to President Barack Obama after the passage of the Affordable Care Act, and as quaint as *tits* may now seem on Carlin's list, characters on television still use it much less than their real-life equivalents. *Boobs* is one thing—we're not surprised to hear it on *Modern Family* despite the fact that no one would have said it on *All in the Family*. But *tits*, the word used for purposes of lusty appraisal? We still tread lightly. Profanity channels our essence even when eluding logic, even more mysterious in leaving us quaking at the utterance of what are, in the end, just words.

But clearly these aren't "just words" like names of fruits or animals at the zoo. In terms of how we produce them in our brains, curses are indeed different from *boy*, *run*, *already*, and *nevertheless*. In most people, language is generated on the left side of the brain, which is associated with logic, motor functions, the Apollonian realm of things. That's the side that lights up in a PET scan when we speak ordinary words and sentences. However, when we haul off with a curse word, it's parts of the right side that light up—specifically, the areas associated with emotion and calibrating its cathartic expression.

The limbic system, as these parts are called, looks like a graceful coil (often for some reason colored lavender in illustrations), which has always led me to associate it with Princess Leia. The left hemisphere can be entirely removed, which yields two interesting results. The first is being alive—such people can survive. The second is that they can no longer speak in terms of ordinary words and sentences but can still cuss like sailors. Likewise, a person without a right brain can talk up a storm but finds themselves stymied when they try to swear.

This means that when you yell *shit* or *fuck*, you are not simply uttering a "word." Curses erupt from the more emotional, impulsive parts of our brains, more squawks than labels. A word is presented; a curse pops out. Where we have the space to carefully assemble and burnish our sentences, something like *already* or *grocery store* comes out; meanwhile, we spit out *fuck* when it's time to run away from a lion. This is part of why curses can be so utterly disconnected from their technical meanings. In yelling *"Shit!"* when we realize we forgot our phone, we are not likening anything to poop; *"Fuck!"* we say when stubbing

4

our toe, certainly not meaning "Sexual congress!" Curses are clad in the guise of words, like those little chocolate liquor bottles; to approach these with thoughts of Godiva and Russell Stover is missing their point, which is what's sloshing around inside of them.

———

The point, then—the essence—is the piqued sense of offense, and how we cope with that blow via the visceral and immediate gesture of swatting back. You level your revenge by saying something you have been told that you should not. Herein lies profanity's punch. As Carlin deftly got it across, "These words have no power. We give them this power by refusing to be free and easy with them. We give them great power over us. They really, in themselves, have no power." Curses are words that have long ago ceased being themselves, having been vested with the power of transgression. They may have emerged as ordinary words but, over time, they made their way from our left brains to our right.

In the Middle Ages, in England, Bristol's maps showed a glade called Fuckinggrove, while up in Chester one could proudly sport a name like Roger Fuckbythenavel. Only once *fuck* crossed that cognitive boundary a few centuries later did it become a word so dirty that generations of lexicographers pretended that it didn't exist. And just as a word can attain profane status, it can lose it. Going back to Carlin's list, I am pretty sure I have never in my lifetime (which began in 1965) heard anyone called a *cocksucker* and have certainly never leveled the term. In the 1960s and 1970s trailblazing representative Bella Abzug was reportedly fond of it in honest moments as a general term for persons of whom she disapproved, but it seems to have migrated into archaism since then. These days, you're much more likely to hear *asshole*, which settled in as an equivalent term in the late 1960s.

What's key is that the stock of curses is ever self-refreshing. The fashions change, as always and everywhere, but what persists is taboo itself, a universal of human societies. What is considered taboo itself differs from one epoch to another, but the sheer fact of taboo does not. Language cannot help but reflect something so fundamental to our social consciousness, and thus there will always be words and expressions that are shot out of the right brain rather than gift-wrapped by the left one.

This is why they have the peculiar status that George Carlin commented upon—and why, while the potency of much of his list has weakened considerably, new ones have arisen that occupy the same place in the culture. Maybe your aunt Frances walked out of the room rather than listen to Carlin's disquisition when her nephew Craig was playing it on his record player around when Nixon was reelected. But then how many of us would be up for watching a comedian today on Netflix gabbing about how we need to get over our delicate treatment of *nigger* and *faggot*? In fact, Carlin's case that these words "really in themselves have no power" is academic; words like these wield modern America's strongest taboo, the slander of groups. Both words stopped being "themselves" long ago.

Profanity will always intrigue us with its distinctive status and flavor amid the "real" words that make up our language. They are both not real words and realer than most others. What chose them to give vent to our ids? How have our curse words transformed along with our taboos? And what can these words teach us about language and linguistics in general? Just think: *ass* is a pronoun, *fuck* is becoming a question word, and *darn* is no more a "real word" than *ginormous* or *hangry*. There's more to profanity than discomfort, catharsis, and seduction.

As often as not, we will be finding structure in what seems like chaos, mess, or the trivial. That is the heart of what linguistics is, and this will be a linguist's journey through profanity, rather than an anthropologist's, psychologist's, or historian's. So many think that we are translators, or grammar scolds, or experts on how to teach kids to read, or dialect coaches. We are none of those things. Rather, we take in what looks like a mess and try to make out the sense in it. We like to think of ourselves as scientists. Without taking a linguistics class, you can't know that the subject is taught with problem sets of the kind more familiar to physics or statistics. The idea is to find the sense in the chaos.

And the chaos includes matters profane. If you watch shows

like *Succession*—excellent in exhibiting how words like *fuck*, *shit*, and *ass* are used "in the wild" as opposed to on the page—you might figure that we are dirty, profane, and, most to the point here, random. But no—a linguist's view reveals that the casual modern English speaker is as systematic in our language usage as Winston Churchill, Gwendolyn Brooks, or Christopher Hitchens.

In this book I will zero in on not seven but nine of the bedrock swears of modern English, including what we more conventionally term *slurs* but which qualify as our newest profanity. Or, really, eleven if you count *damn* and *hell*. For all that these two are conventionally listed as profane, in modern times, they are better described as salty. They are used too commonly in public and even formal settings to count meaningfully as obscene, especially since they were used rather openly even in early talkie films with their otherwise post-Victorian approach to language. Yet these words were treated as more profane in the deeper past, and in this, illustrate an entire stage in the evolution of what Anglophones consider obscene that would be lost if we just started with the likes of *shit*. Add that sheer habit leads us to spontaneously include *damn* and *hell* on the "bad word" list and even lead that list off with them in our minds, and I would be not only pedagogically irresponsible but a wet blanket to disinclude them from this book. Thus we will start off with them as a kind of prologue chapter, separate from what truly constitute our nasty words.

On that matter of evolution, profanity has known three

main eras—when the worst you could say was about religion, when the worst you could say was about the body, and when the worst you could say was about groups of people. The accumulation of those taboos is why "just words" like *hell*, *shit*, and *nigger* respectively harbor such sting. Onlookers have sucked in their breath to hear the medieval person damning someone to hell, the twenties flapper telling someone to go fuck themselves, and our neighbor calling someone a bitch. This book will explain why.

But more to the point, this book is all about the words themselves. Not every single cuss we can name, though—do you really need a list of *all* the words for *penis*? We're going to work with a lean list of the staple, principal-cast dirty words you giggled at when you learned them as a kid, the words you want to know when learning a second language, and the ones you hope your kids won't use, and yet you would never feel your full self without deploying a few of now and then. To wit—and hopefully with some of it—let's look in for a spell on nine nasty ways of being human.

1

DAMN AND *HELL*:
ENGLISH'S FIRST BAD WORDS

In a book about profanity, it's almost awkward that our tour begins with *damn* and *hell*, in that most of us don't sense these words as truly, well, dirty.

We may still include both in a standard list of "four-letter words" formally classified as unsuitable for the drawing room. For many, *damn* is the first we might list, just as we are likely to start with apples when asked to name fruits. We sense *damn*, as well as *hell*, as in some sense "bad."

Yet in our times, they really aren't.

The Cusses That Aren't

When I was about eight, I asked my father what *dam-un* meant, assuming that was how one pronounced the *damn* I had seen in writing. Dad said, "It's a word you use when you're really, really angry."

The result was that I went away supposing for years afterward that there was a word *dam* that you used as a kind of everyday, salty exclamation, and a less commonly used word pronounced *dam-un* that you used when truly irritated.

That is, I was well aware of the word that sounds like *dam*, as the one bandied about quite often by my parents and others, even when kids were within earshot, for reasons much less extreme than being "really, really angry." In no sense did I classify it as an especially naughty word, even if I knew that I wasn't allowed to say it yet.

Gradually, of course, I realized that there was no separate word *dam-un*. But the gap between my dad's formal parsing of the word, as a genuine obscenity, and the libertine reality of how he—and even President Nixon, as we'd learn—used it was instructive. For an obscenity, *damn*, like *hell*, was used with curious comfort and frequency.

Nor was this freedom a product of the countercultural 1960s, after which we all let our hair down in so many ways. My father was born in 1927, and Richard Nixon was not exactly a flower child. *Damn* and *hell* have been profanity-lite for a very long time.

As far back as the 1880s, publishing magnate Joseph Pulitzer (whose name appears during my typical workday not once but twice in being doughtily imprinted upon both Columbia University's journalism school building as well as a public school I live near) was known to favor *damn*. He was especially fond of jamming it into words that hadn't expected it, in a fashion more familiar today with locutions such as "abso-fucking-lutely," resulting in the likes of "indegoddampendent." A young woman recounting her spell as an itinerant in the teens of the twentieth century noted that *damn* and *hell* were ordinary talk among her fellow hobos but that they carefully shielded her from other, "real" bad words.

But what about the hubbub surrounding *Gone with the Wind*? The truth is, producer David O. Selznick was *not* fined for instructing Clark Gable as Rhett Butler to say, "Frankly, my dear, I don't give a damn." The post–Victorian Motion Picture Production Code of the era had indeed forbidden profanity on film for several years by 1939, but Selznick got it altered, without any major trouble, on *damn* and *hell*. The update nicely reflected the twentieth-century reality, allowing those two words:

> *when their use shall be essential and required for portrayal, in proper historical context, of any scene or dialogue*

based upon historical fact or folklore… or a quotation from a literary work, provided that no such use shall be permitted which is intrinsically objectionable or offends good taste.

Moreover, the line was nowhere near the first time *damn* had been uttered on film. Given how linguistically puritan American film producers generally kept their output until the late 1960s, it is almost bizarre how free with *damn* and *hell* some early talkies were. As soon as sound came in, profanity hit the ground running, spoken by pomaded post-Victorians in their fussy clothing. In 1929, the creaky slog of a musical *Glorifying the American Girl* has a crabby stage mother casually grunting "Dammit!" twice, as she has trouble opening her glasses. In 1932, a sweet, matronly figure casually says, "I'll be damned!" in *Blessed Event*. Even cartoon characters got in on the action. Flip the Frog was one of many Mickey Mouse knockoffs of the era, as evanescent as they were inevitable, and in one 1930 entry, an anthropomorphic telephone tries unsuccessfully to wake up Flip and looks at the audience and whispers "Damn!" in frustration.

To wit, since the late nineteenth century, *damn* and *hell* have been understood as inappropriate in a formulaic sense, while in everyday life many "proper" people have treated them like cinnamon sticks in tea. By the time we got to 1977, when Florida Evans, the staid matriarch of *Good Times*, cried,

"Damn, damn, *damn*!" after her husband died in a car accident, we neither batted an eye nor wished she had said, "Darn, darn, *darn*!"

The Way We Were

Damn and *hell* were once more potent. As with profanity in all societies, the words were never anywhere near absent from ordinary speech, as their taboo status inevitably lent satisfaction to their utterance and lent them a space within the full range of human expression. The difference between then and now was the genuflection to that forbidden status one was expected to maintain, the studious display of disgust. They truly qualified as "bad" words, however commonly they were heard.

As in: it isn't hard to glean that premarital sex was common before the pill. Any number of clues tip us off—the date of first children's birthdays, deathbed confessions, widespread venereal disease, the sheer existence of prophylactic devices. It is equally easy to see that public attitudes about it were quite different from private ones, about those who ventured the deed without "benefit of clergy."

An analogous split between public ideals and private reality is the source of our hangover sense even today that there is something unclean about *damn* and *hell*. But people maintained the pretense much more vigorously a century or so ago.

Whatever Pulitzer was shouting in his shirtsleeves in the smoky just-the-boys atmosphere of his office, in the Gilded Age there was a sense that *damn* and *hell* had no place in one's public persona.

Gilbert and Sullivan's *H.M.S. Pinafore* number "I am the Captain of the Pinafore" summed it up when the captain informs us:

> *Bad language or abuse*
> *I never, never use*
> *Whatever the emergency.*
> *Though "bother it" I may*
> *Occasionally say,*
> *I never use a big, big D____.*

"What, never?" the chorus asks.

"No, never!" he answers.

"What, never?" the chorus pushes, upon which he admits, "Hardly ever!" So one was to at least tamp it down. Even as late as 1935, Thomas Edison's erstwhile assistant Miller Hutchison was eliding the *hell*s in letters in a similar fashion, quoting his old boss as having said in 1915: "I want to be able to tell an Admiral to go to _____ if he is in the wrong."

This gingerly approach was more about etiquette-book stipulation than reality, but the stipulation itself contrasted with our times.

Frank Lloyd Wright urged that in architecture, form follows

function but was hardly consistent about it. Sometimes he pursued a form because he felt like it. Regarding his gorgeous but weirdly laid-out Unity Church in Oak Park, Illinois, around 1905, he groused to a colleague, "I don't give a damn what the use of it is; I wanted to build a building like that." Wright's contemporary equivalent would use in the same place *shit* or *fuck*—i.e., what we think of as "real" profanity.

Another revealing facet: *damn* and *hell* were considered vulgar enough—"on paper" at least—that bourgeois propriety enforced a distinct gender segregation. In 1861, poet Algernon Swinburne wrote a letter to a woman where he wrote that certain scenery was "of the sort which must be called, not in the way of profane swearing, but of grave, earnest and sorrowing indignation, the d____ sort." He appended, "I wd. rather die than write it at length." Here, then, is the kind of context where, as late as the 1910s, cartoonist Art Young would describe Greenwich Village as where "a woman could say *damn* right out loud and still be respected!"—i.e., notably bohemian.

This had been the general Anglophone sentiment on the two words since their emergence in Old English more than a thousand years before, and nothing testifies to this more vividly than that English has long had euphemisms for both, such as *darn*, *doggone*, *dang*, *heck*, and *H-E-double-hockey-sticks*. The prolificity of these prim little terms only makes sense amid a widespread sense that *damn* and *hell* are not just ordinary words but taboo terms—like *Voldemort*. We have no substitutes for *snow*, *yesterday*, or *kitchen sink*.

When Swearing Was Swearing

This diligent euphemizing goes back to the ancients, for whom the rub was what they considered most taboo in contrast to us. Namely, it came down to the issue of swearing.

Hold up: Swearing is what this whole book is about, right? But our use of *swear* as a synonym for profanity is actually a holdover from an earlier usage that made more sense. After all, one might ask just what swearing in its literal meaning—affirming your belief in something—has to do with what you yell when you stub your toe. To the medievals, swearing was about swearing—in the actual sense—to God and Jesus, and was taken seriously to an extent difficult for most of us to wrap our heads around today.

I got my first sense of this from Peter Shaffer's play *Lettice and Lovage*, lesser known than his *Amadeus* and *Equus* but just as substantial (and funnier). Lettice is a woman of a certain age with a theatrical temperament and an antiquarian bent, who resists being dismissed from a job as a tour guide in a medieval castle.

> I swear—I swear to you—if I can do this job, I shall not deviate by so much as a syllable from the re-corded truth!… I shall read and read! I shall commit to memory every recorded fact about the river! I shall not depart from them by so much as one cedilla—not

a jot or tittle! Not one iota!... *[Lettice tears the property sword off the wall and kneels, holding it up ardently.]*

I swear this!... Not one complaint will you hear! Not a single—not a single—a sing— *[breaks down in tears]*

Doing this bit in the original production, Maggie Smith struck a knightlike pose delightfully out of step with her dowdy puff of a coiffure and loopy attire. In a later repertory production I caught, the magnificent Tina Packer knelt down, opened her mouth in a froglike gape, and shouted the line bug-eyed to an imaginary audience, as if she were an actual medieval person swearing before gathered witnesses in the open air, yelling to be heard in an era before amplification.

To the ancients, swearing actually was this weighted and performative. In societies where language was mainly oral and few were literate, the swear was equivalent to the signature, and thus to do it without sincerity threatened the foundations of society. Swearing insincerely to God was especially egregious. To swear to God for trivial reasons, or worse, disingenuously, was regarded as morally repellent at best, sinful at worst. Here emerged the condemnation of taking the Lord's name "in vain." Other transgressions were calling upon God to damn someone, or taking a personal role in the direction of someone to reside in hell, when that assignment is God's decision to make.

Hence the idea that certain words and expressions constitute "swearing"—this is why an alternate term is *oaths*. The original literalness and sincerity becomes clear in now frozen expressions such as *oh God, thank God, my God, swear to God, honest to God, for God's sake, God forbid, good God, by God,* and *so help me, God.* One might imagine how someone who uses these expressions in earnest might feel about someone tossing them off to release steam. Not for nothing is the instruction to avoid taking the Lord's name in vain the second of the Commandments, before murder and adultery.

Perhaps the closest we can get to this kind of sentiment is being *sworn in* in court, where we give oral promise to be truthful and it is considered illegal not to. While today that practice stands out as singular, even odd, the old sense of *damn* and *hell* as evil was rooted in a world in which swearing of this kind was part of the warp and woof of life, crucial to situating oneself in a community or society.

Thus our use of "swearing" to refer to something considered transgressive is a faded signal from a distant era when swearing itself was fine and even advisable: the issue was how you did it. Hence Swinburne's careful assurance to his interlocutor, before he describes something as *damned,* that he does not intend the *profane* kind of swearing—i.e., he thought the scenery was genuinely revolting. Swearing was a problem only when people did it too lightly. Or too often—no circumstances justified swearing to or about the Lord as a kind of punctuation day in and day out. This is what rankles Chaucer's

Pardoner in the *Canterbury Tales*, who teaches that while sincere swearing is proper, "ydel swerying"—*ydel* is *idle*—"is a cursednesse."

Damning people to hell was but one manifestation of this devaluation. Another one, more often remarked upon in the Middle Ages, was swearing to parts of God's and Jesus's bodies. Here were now archaic-sounding eruptions such as *by God's nails*, *by God's arms*, and *by his* (i.e., Jesus's) *wounds*, considered reprehensible in dividing God and Jesus into parts. "O wickedness! O abomination! What parts of Christ's most blessed body do these wicked and abominable swearers leave unrent and untorn?" asked proselytizing preacher Thomas Becon in the sixteenth century, while around the same time diplomat Sir Thomas Elyot wrote in despair that children "do play with the armes and bones of Christe, as they were chery stones." These expressions were especially on the mind of Chaucer's Pardoner:

> *vengeance shal nat parten* [leave] *from his hous*
> *That* [he who] *of his othes* [oaths] *is to* [too] *outrageous.*

As in, those who cuss too freely better watch out for the torture of vengeance. The Pardoner continues by aping such persons:

> *"By Goddes precious herte,"* and *"By his nayles,"*
> *And "By the blood of Crist that is in Hayles* [Hales Abbey],

Sevene is my chaunce, and thyn is cynk and treye [five
  and three]!"
"By Goddes armes, if thou falsly pleye,
This daggere shal thurghout thyn herte go!"

Lexical Fig Leaves

Today, the body-part swears are more familiar from their eu-
phemizations than their original renditions, which speaks to
the revulsion that once surrounded them. *Zounds* is from *by his*
wounds, from when *wound* in reference to injury was still pronounced as the past tense of the verb *wind* as in what you do to
a watch. I'm not sure anyone still says *gadzooks*, but it was from
God's hooks—the nails used in Jesus's crucifixion. We can see
Odds bodkins emerging from "God's body" in Shakespeare:
Henry IV, Part II has a line "God's body! The turkeys in my pan-
nier are quite starved." (It's not one of Shakespeare's more iconic
lines.) The Bard added the "cutesifying" suffix *-kin* later when
Hamlet says, "God's bodykins, man, much better. Use every
man after his desert, and who should 'scape whipping?" Leaving
off the *g* and *y*, then, yields the queer little locution *Odds bod-*
kins! we now vaguely associate with men in stockings fencing
on staircases (or at least I do).

The names of God and Jesus, too, have been fertile sources
for these kinds of euphemisms. *Golly* and *gosh* emerged as ways
to avoid taking God's name in vain while still spritzing out a bit

of amazement or disgust. *Goodness*, and variants such as *Goodness gracious*, emerged for the same reason—the goodness and grace in question are the essences of God. The British *Cor blimey!* started as *Gor blimey*, which was a disguised "God blind me," as in "May God blind me if...," a "swear," as it were.

Cripes gave the same treatment to Christ, and *Jeepers creepers!* seems less goofy when we realize it was a way of not saying Jesus Christ. We hardly, if at all, associate *gee* with *Jesus!*, although the fact that *jeez* is an alternate gives a clue. *Jesus* has had other lexical offspring: rather than saying "Jee-*ziss*!" one might say—or did in the nineteenth century and possibly before—"Gee whiz!"

Whether *gee whillikers* and *gee willikins* emerged to further cloak the source word or out of verbal playfulness *à la* the progression of *yes, sir* to *yessiree* to the yippingly meaningless *yessireebob* is anyone's guess. Clearer, though, is that lately, Anglophones have increasingly gone directly to the fount. The *gosh* school of interjections feel, to many, more juice-and-cookies by the year, in contrast to just naming God and Jesus outright. This parallels the fate of public attitudes about *damn* and *hell*: we have ever less sense of a lexical taboo on religion. One academic study tracked casual English over a hundred years showing that the grand old euphemisms started losing ground to, especially, *oh my God* starting in the 1930s, with the erosion really settling in, as we would expect, after the 1960s.

Like many hit television shows, *All in the Family* ran too long, and in the fashion of sitcoms of the period, someone decided to spark things up by introducing a cute kid. Hence Archie and Edith took in a niece. The actress, Danielle Brisebois, was farmed out to make appearances on other shows, one of which was a game show I caught, circa 1978. As the host presented her prize, Brisebois exclaimed "Oh my God!" multiple times. I remember cringing, thinking that no one had told the poor girl not to take the Lord's name in vain on TV—I had once or twice been called out for doing so by my more religious relatives.

What I didn't know was that Brisebois was part of a change in progress, now iconicized in popular culture by, for example, the musical *Legally Blonde*, which opens with the number "Omigod You Guys," sung by mostly white sisters. It manages to perfectly summon a stylized version of how this cohort speaks, including how, and how often, they say "Oh my God!" Believe it or not, the way we linguists know that "Oh my God!" has really set into society at large is that white women, like Brisebois, have deployed this change the most.

What, why? Because: when men's speech differs from women's, it tends to be in terms of the colloquial, vulgar even— *singin'* instead of *singing*. Our sense of what is "proper" has a way of keeping things like that from becoming accepted as standard. In contrast, when women's speech differs from men's, it tends to be in below-the-radar ways, driven by the fact that human speech is dynamic in the same way as clouds always change shape. It was women who quietly started saying *talks* and *has* rather than *talketh* and *hath*, until after a while, with no one having had much to say about it, the old -*th* ending was antique.

Women have likewise been in the vanguard on expressions like *oh my God*—note that this probably feels intuitive despite that you likely never had occasion to think about it—and that's a sign that we are truly sidelining *gosh* and *golly* and *gee*. This got Mitt Romney, who favors what we might call the g-words, in trouble when he ran for president. Romney's Mormon faith still discourages taking God's name in vain, so he was given to saying things like "This was back, oh gosh, probably in the late seventies," or when asked whether his religion might be a disadvantage, "Gee, I hope not"; elsewhere speculating, "Oh, I think, initially, some people would say, 'Gosh, I don't know much about your faith, tell me about it.'" To voters in 1950, Romney's delicacy would have sounded appropriately "presidential." In 2012, he sounded like Ned Flanders on *The Simpsons*.

———

Damn and *hell*, then, are two tokens within a general trend. Into the sixteenth century, the sense of taboo we today feel about terms relating to the body and sex applied instead to matters of religion. Damning, and the place one was usually damned to, was taken literally. Thus a question as to why *damn* and *hell* are bad words reveals them to have undergone the same drift from a more logical treatment. In the 500s CE, Pope Gregory commanded his subjects to say "God bless you" when someone sneezed because it was often the first sign of being infected with plague. Today, we say it as a rigorously policed and yet vacuous courtesy. Just how vacuous, I got a sense of when I knew someone who had never learned the courtesy and would just sit there like a bump on a log after I sneezed. The impossibility of explaining "why" she should say "God bless you" quickly revealed what a knee-jerk tradition it is. For most of us, *damn* and *hell* are as disconnected from their initial meaning as *God bless you* is from a concern about pestilence and boils. All that remains is the gestural.

One *Damn* Thing After Another

One might have a sense that the etymology of curse words will be as spicy as their usage, but where *damn* is concerned that isn't the case. The original word was Latin's *damnare*, meaning "to condemn" and pronounced "dom-NAH-ray," passed on to English through French's version of that word, *damner* ("dom-NAY"). English took that in as *damnen*—at first, "DOM-nun"—and as was its wont, dumped the unaccented second syllable, which left just "dom," which eventually was pronounced "dam." But there were, especially around the time of the Renaissance, ever certain nudgy scribal sorts, their names lost to history, insisting that English spelling was better off retaining lookbacks to earlier stages of pronunciation, often in other languages. Hence today's confusing *damn* with it considered louche to spell it *dam*, as it is pronounced.

As Kurt Vonnegut would have put it, "So it goes." And as it did, with *damn* first referring to a curse and the action of leveling it, as in *God damn that man*, eventually economy provided the simple *Damn!* Not only the utterance itself but also its meaning abbreviated—focused, even. What began as a command to condemn, already an emotional one venturing a certain amount of right-brain real estate, became a mere bark of annoyance, now settled in the right brain for real and for good.

But even if we can't trace *damn* to some fascinatingly alternate meaning ("It used to mean to tickle!") or counterintuitively distant source ("It's actually from Tibetan!"), it can still delight. Curse words have a way of encouraging fanciful etymologies, and *damn* is no exception. *Fuck* is supposedly an acronym for fornication under consent of the king, and *shit* is said to have begun as an acronym warning sailors not to stock their ships with manure on the lowest deck (we'll get back to that one in chapter three).

Damn's legend is cuter—the dām was a currency of India when the British colonized it, and this is said to be where the expression "I don't give a dam[n]" began, when administrators and soldiers brought it back to England. Folk etymologies like this, however, often reveal themselves as folk in certain implausibilities. It is a bit of a stretch to imagine that the countless millions of Brits who had not been to India would pick up on a weird idiom some dads and uncles and brothers were dropping around, especially not knowing themselves what a dām even was. (Imagine your father returning from Kazakhstan fond of saying, "I don't give a tenge whether we have dessert or not!"— how likely would you be to start saying it?) Besides, the Raj was centuries later than Old and Middle English, where *damn* was already long established in its meaning of condemnation and diminishment.

Multiple causation beckons as always, in courteously allowing everyone their say. As such, we might venture that the angry, dismissive feel of *damn* encouraged the use of the Indian word because of its similar sound—comparing something to a sweaty little metal dām felt right because *damn* already conveyed a contemptuous wave of the arm. But even that account isn't necessary. Way back in Middle English, people were all but saying "I don't give a damn" already: *Piers Plowman* has "Wisdom and wit is not now worth a curse" as far back as 1377. The English were likening curses to worthlessness long before any of them had even heard of India.

Another neat idea rolls off into the same gutter—that *I don't give a damn* began as *I don't give a tinker's dam*. This time the *dam* in question is not a coin but perhaps even more obscure, a kind of temporary caulking that tinkers (i.e., menders of metal) once used during repair, of a nature so mind-numbingly particular that we need not dwell on it here except to note that this "dam" was discarded after the job was done and thus worthless. But the typical medieval English person was neither a tinker nor married or related to one. Plus, page a little further back in time and the expression is recorded also as *tinker's curse*. The dam was the swear *damn*, not the lumpy ring of crud in the dumpster.

Damn also provides a fine lesson in that eternal difference between what people think they are like and what they actually do, the gulf between the rules and the reality, as in why no one talks about how Junior was born six months after Mommy and Daddy tied the knot. Consider the Zelig-like quality of *goddamn*, the package in which *damn* comes as often as not. We can't hear how ordinary people spoke until recordings of the twentieth century, and thus for the most part our reconstruction of who used profanity and how much before that relies on what reached the page. Luckily, some deductions can get us close to the real thing.

Nothing, for example, makes it clearer how incessantly *damn* was used way back than learning that to foreigners, *goddamn* was as much the essence of the English language and soul as *Oh là là!* seems to us as the essence of Frenchness. In fact, Joan of Arc called English people "Goddams," as did a great many of her compatriots. In the 1820s, a Hawaiian native who had picked up some English greeted a debarking captain with "Glad to see you! Damn your eyes! Me like English very much. Devilish hot, sir! Goddam!" And none other than Voltaire, whose English had gotten shaky by late in his life, once ventured, "I do love the Ingles God dammee."

Voltaire's "dammee" isn't a foreigner's flub à la "I no speakee English." *Damn me* was once a prevalent expression (*fuck me* has since usurped it) that served, like *goddamn*, as a label for entire groups of people. Oliver Cromwell's Roundheads were known to call the royalist Cavaliers "Dammees." *Damn* was like a stutter in the mitochondrial DNA of the Anglophone context, carried along even by people dimly aware of its meaning if at all, but ever revealing that word as part of the genuine entirety of the lexicon, appearances be, well, damned.

The paces that English puts *damn* through are rather astounding. *Darn*, for example, is not a random fudging but a downright game-of-telephone mangling of what began as *By the eternal!* as a euphemism for *by the eternal God*. There were those who were given to pronouncing the word *etarnal*, for the same reason that they might say "larn" for learn—or, for that matter, pronounce *concern* as "consarn" in *Consarn it!*, yet another euphemism for *goddamnit*. That *etarnal* shortened, naturally, to *tarnal*. Because this was a substitute for *damn*, it was equally natural to assume subconsciously that if there is a word *damnation* there is a word *tarnation*—and soon, there was. From here, it was a short step to imagining that if *damnation* had its *damn*, then *tarnation* had its *tarn*, or, since what we really have in mind is a way of saying *damn* without saying it and *damn* begins with d, *darn*.

Few etymologies rival this one in the contrast between the

beginning and the end, such as the origins of *bye* in *God be with you*. We got from the four words of *by the eternal God* to the single caw of *darn* by six processes operating in succession.

STAGE	PROCESS	AS IN . . .
By the eternal!	euphemization	*Jesus!* > *Jeepers!*
Ternal!	erosion	*God be with you* > *Bye*
Tarnal!	sound change	*learn* > "larn"
Tarnation!	blending	*breakfast* + *lunch* > *brunch*
Darn!	analogy	"yourn" and "hisn" because of *mine*
Darn! (sweetie)	devernacularization	*veggie* c. 1980 > *veggie burger*

Note the last change, where *darn* goes from low-class to "presentable." *Darn* began with a certain air of the *yeehaw!* about it just as *veggie* was once something one only said to infants and toddlers. *Tarnal!* was favored by Andrew Jackson, and fairly dripped from depictions of uncultivated American male speech of the early nineteenth century. Today, though, *darn* is less about "tobacky" than avocado toast. If anything, we all give in to a good *damn* when needed. It has been reassigned in the sociological sense, now vanilla English rather than a colloquialism associated with the Frontier or, really, the anything.

Doggone, dang—as in, *damn* masked by *hang* as in *hang it all*—and the Black American *Dag!* all disguise *damn* while leaving it recognizable, via coy sound changes. *Drat* seems like it should belong to this family, too, but emerged via a separate transformation, from *God rot*. Elsewhere Anglophones have subbed in similarly curt, monosyllabic words that get across the idea. In the old *Sad Sack* comic books about a feckless, miserable soldier during World War II, I was intrigued to see the grouchy Sarge yelling "Blast!" in situations that, in my adolescent opinion, called for a *damn*. *Blast* (or *blast it*) was in fact used a fair amount in the early twentieth century and before— some may also recall it from Fred MacMurray's Mr. Biddle in the film *The Happiest Millionaire*, which was set in 1916 and, in this at least, reflected the reality of the period.

A Visit to *Hell*

The word *hell* traces to an Old English one that paralleled the Greek *hades* and the Hebrew Bible's *sheol*, and then back to an earlier one, in the ancestor to almost all European languages, that meant "cover." That word morphed not only into *hell*, but *hall*, *hole*, and *hollow*, but also *ceiling*, *cell*, *conceal*, and *kleptomania*. All suggest elements of covering, but only knowing that the *h* of *hell* began as a *k* makes the likeness between, say, *hell* and *cell* evident. That original word also spawned the name William—which arose as Wilhelm, with *-helm* coming from *helmet*, a kind of covering.

Like *damn*, *hell* has long been a bad word in name only. As early as 1932, cartoon characters were using it—they weren't "real" enough to be subject to the language taboos of the culture at large—when, in another weird Flip the Frog short, a horse sings a lyric containing the word. Flip smacks him over the head for the transgression, to be sure, but still—the horse said it. Even in the Eisenhower 1950s, Rodgers and Hammerstein had no problem with frustrated Chinese elders singing, in "The Other Generation" in their musical *Flower Drum Song*, that they hoped their children's children would give their parents the same "hell" they had given them.

But these are twentieth-century stories. A bit earlier there would have been no doubt that *hell* was profane. In 1834, Irish author William Maginn pirouetted nicely around it in his short story "Bob Burke's Duel with Ensign Brady of the 48th":

"I will," said I at once, and left the house in the most abrupt manner, after consigning Ensign Brady to the particular attention of Tisiphone, Alecto, and Megaera, all compressed into one emphatic monosyllable.

Tisiphone, Alecto, and Megaera are the Furies of Greek mythology, who live more or less in hell, so we can assume that Mr. Brady was instructed to go there.

Writers had not always been so shy about writing it out. In 1600, Shakespeare had Portia say, "Let fortune go to hell for it, not I" in *The Merchant of Venice*, with Ben Jonson two years later chiming in with "The hell thou wilt, what, turne Law into verse?" in *Poetaster*. But the flowering of bourgeois senses of propriety among Anglophone readers in the eighteenth century encouraged the hyphenization of *hell*, with a tacit idea that it was only proper to spell out generally when uttered by men, often either military or "backwoods," sounding off in dramatic circumstances. In 1914, the *Chicago Examiner* described a man about to expire from suicide as groaning "To h—l with it," euphemized even in the mental anguish of his last words. It isn't an accident that the earliest known written attestation of the simple exclamation "Hell!" happens to be someone in the late nineteenth century complaining about how some people pop off with it much too often.

Film producers after the Production Code were even primmer about *hell* than publishers, as movies were more widely distributed than books, and a "hotter," more immediate medium. As late as 1943's *Yankee Doodle Daffy*, Daffy Duck accidentally missiles himself into the underworld and, suddenly in the red, flaming world of the devil, gasps, "This place looks like (eech!)... Hey, it *is* (eech, ugh!)... I *am* in (gulp!)"—never nailing the word, even just to describe the actual place. In more than one thousand shorts from 1930 to 1969, no Looney Tunes character, as randy and colloquial as they were, ever said *hell*.

Hence as rich a euphemization for this word as for *damn*. Something about *heck*, especially, elicits an entertaining array of wobbly origin stories. I've heard that a word that pops up around the time of the Civil War somehow got to America on the lips of countryfolk from northern England—i.e., that undocumented yet massive wave of Yorkshiremen who were

attracted to the wreck of a nation just past the devastating con-
flagration of the massive recession that broke out a few years
after it—and then, unlike any other words they used, was adopted and spread throughout the entire United States!

Or it began as the name of an Icelandic volcano that witches
inhabited in legend, so eagerly recounted as all Nordic epics are
on these American shores and into its heartland. Or as the
name of one of a loom's small parts ("Oh, *crankshaft*!"). Or just
maybe, *heck* is an echo of people who actually wanted to shout
"By Hector!" (Hector is whom, exactly?)

Or maybe—i.e., really—*heck* is just a random distortion like
the equally cuteish *gosh*, *shyte*, and *fudge*. One now obsolete
alternate is *hay*, most memorably associated with old-time bur-
lesque comedians. In line with a rule that they keep their language clean—*cheese and crackers!* was for *Jesus Christ!*—they
said, *What the hay?!* (a lot) for *What the hell?!** Daffy Duck
edged a little closer to *hell* than he did in *Yankee Doodle Daffy*
when in *Rabbit Seasoning* (1952) he chirped, planting signs
pointing hunters to Bugs Bunny's burrow, "What the hay, I gotta
have *some* fun!" *What the deuce?* emerged because in cards,
number two—*deuce*—comes from the early French *deus*, which

---

*This usage is preserved in the antics of Phil Silvers and his gang in the Broadway musi-
cal *Top Banana* from 1951. You can get it either through the movie—it was filmed right
onstage—or the cast album, an under-consulted but deft recording from which the
show just jumps out at you with all of its charm and energy. Listen to the title song "Top
Banana."

was associated with bad luck and, pertinently, the devil because it was the lowest score.

———

But English's 2.0 treatments of *hell* are especially fun. Words that we use a lot have a way of drifting, and not just in the way that *head* can refer to a literal body part or the metaphorical "head" of something. Rather, a word can start out meaning something concrete and end up a bit of grammar—a prefix, a suffix, or even a tone, some blip, whose relationship to the original word, a free-standing, breathing, parseable thing, is all but unrecoverable.

Take *let's*: we know from the spelling that the *'s* comes from *us*. This means that a pronoun *us*, with the "real article" job of referring to two or more people, is now just a sound. The sound serves to indicate "Here's what we should do." *'T's try to get to get there early when the food is hotter*—that little *'s* does the job and sounds not at all like *us*. In *let's*, even the speaker's own involvement in the action can now be an abstraction, which is clear in the slangy *'T's you and him fight*, which summons a fight in which *you*, despite being part of the implied *us*, do not intend to participate. The *'s* salutes the fact that you are invested in the fight happening and will enjoy seeing it. The *we*-ness is an echo, a falsity, even.

One could never have known, when in *let* the *us* meant "we," that it would drift down a pathway to render it a mere marker of grammar—the hortatory, or what you can just think of as vastly distinct from a pronoun. In the same way, the adverbial -*ly* once meant, of all things, *body*! Curse words, heavily used, have a way of developing sideline usages awesomely unlike anything you'd have predicted, and *hell* is fun in that way.

Consider *even*—not in the sense of flatness, nor as opposite to *odd*, but as in *I would even play the maid*. What does *even* "mean" there? That's a tough one to get across to a curious second-language English speaker, and merely saying, "It puts emphasis on something" doesn't cut it. You don't mean "What I said was, I would play the *maid*, not the mailman." You mean something more nuanced than that.* It's a kind of word that indicates background statements not being expressed overtly. A great deal of casual communication is like that. *I would even play the maid* "means" that:

A. You would happily play the lead.

B. You would happily be the costar.

C. You would happily be the comic relief.

but, contrary to expectation,

D. You would also play the maid.

---

*I was frustrated but empathetic when asking Mandarin speakers some years ago what *jiù* (就) means: "Um… it's just emphasis"—it just didn't help! You have to get a feel for it, which I imagine Chinese learners of English are told about *even*.

Here is the source of that sense that *even* is about "emphasis," and we are indeed stressing that we would be satisfied playing a largely nonspeaking walk-on part. But it's an emphasis that, as well, points silently but directly to an unstated hierarchy of less interesting alternatives.

A question, though, is how a language indicates this nuance. All languages do—it's part of human cognition to want to get across that someone did this, did that, and even did *that*, despite what you'd expect. Yet there is never any single, obvious word that serves no purpose except to convey that concept, in the way that there are such words for *run* and *bone*. Rather, a language has to grab something that is already busy meaning something else, and knead it into meaning "even" as a sideline. Other languages have shanghaied all manner of material to serve the function. German uses "also only" (*auch nur*); Russian does "yeah and" (*da i*); one way Mandarin does it is by saying, roughly, "quite a bit and up to" (*shènzhì*). In other languages, the logic is harder to glean because the game of telephone has been going on so long it's hard to know how it all started. Irish uses "self"—probably as in "the thing itself," as in "even that thing"; French uses "same" (whatever). And oddest of all, English uses a word that refers to the underworld.

Think about it. *I would even play the maid*: note that you can convey the exact same meaning, differing only in flavor, with *Hell, I'd play the maid*. It's that same hierarchy—you'd star, costar, yell "What the hay?" when somebody smacked a pie in your face, or, hell, you'd play the maid.* In colloquial English, *hell* is not only a curse word but also what linguists call a scalar particle.

It's a process that, like the one that affixed *us* to *let*, wore the new little package down to *let's*, and then sanded things down further to *'s*—all to gather a group together to do something.

STEP ONE: *Hell* begins as somewhere you wish persons or things to go when, as my father had it about "dam-un," you're very, very angry.

STEP TWO: Just uttering *hell* becomes a shorthand way of indicating anger of a kind that makes you want to break things, such as rules about using religious language.

STEP THREE: Its force weakens even further, now just carrying a certain insouciance, as in saying "To hell with the proprieties."

STEP FOUR: It becomes a natural preface to expressing something that pushes boundaries, as in the course of running conversation with sentences you use *even* in. *Hell, I'd even clean their blinds if I were allowed to*

---

*Sondheim fans, yes, the line is technically "Heck, I'd even play the maid," and yes, I got the idea to use that sentence playing *Follies* for my girls in the car. ("Yes" as if any of you spontaneously reconstructed that particular scenario!) But the point is that you can take out the *even* and it means the same thing.

spend the night under those fluffy sheets. Hell, I'd even
play the maid.

STEP FIVE: But here, we have redundancy—*hell* and *even*
are conveying the same thing. And *hell* "pops" more,
which means that what's next is *hell, I'd play the*
maid—upon which a word has gone from meaning the
fiery pits to meaning "here's just *how* much."

It's this sort of thing that makes language change become a
spectator sport for linguists rather than the tale of woe and deg-
radation we are so often taught it is. Yoga moms, not just sailors,
are covered in tattoos. Toddlers ask for edamame and pad thai
instead of SpaghettiOs. *Hell* becomes a scalar particle. Language, like life, is this.

As is *hell* coming to mean "in extreme fashion," as in *he ran*
like hell. Languages have fun with how they connote "extremely." Sometimes it makes sense—Mandarin's *jíle* means
"went to the extreme point." Other languages are funkier. In
Saramaccan, spoken in the Surinamese rain forest and created
only a few centuries ago by descendants of slaves who combined
English, Portuguese, Dutch, and two African languages, Fongbe
and Kikongo, one of the ways of conveying the same evaluation
is "to the point that I was happy." English is creative, too, in using "like hell." Whether you danced till you were happy or
danced in a fashion suggesting a temperature akin to the place
the devil resides, the vividness of human speech shines through.

One more: *What the hell is that?* If language is all about

parts of speech, what's *hell* in that sentence? Okay, *hell* is a noun in itself—but here, to what person, place, thing, or concept does it refer? In *get the hell out*, you might venture that *the hell* is an adverb "modifying" *get*. But "Get out 'the-hell'-ly?"—really? That's an odd kind of an adverb, and would we ever say, "Get, in a 'the-hell' fashion"? Precisely which manner of getting, or doing anything, does *the hell* refer to? In any case, back to *What the hell is that?—what* isn't a verb and so the whole adverb issue falls away, and yet clearly we are dealing with the same *the hell*.

Here, *hell* is an interjection that busts up a sentence in the same way that *goddamn* busts up a word like *inde-goddam-pendent*. The question is why. *Hell, what is that?* would be one thing. But what wedged *hell* into the middle of a sentence, in a way that resists any traditional sense of grammatical analysis? Once again, it's a matter of things happening step by step. One day a dinosaur has a bit of fur. Fast-forward and the fur has become ugly filamentous protofeathers to help its descendants keep warm. Fast-forward again and the offspring dinosaurs have outright plumage, serving as sexual advertisement and maybe helping with some kind of clumsy "gliding." Finally, certain dinosaurs are using feathers to spend their lives in the air as what we call birds.

So, one day English speakers are saying, "What in the world is that?" It was likely as far back as Old English, as even King Alfred wrote in a poem, "Who in the world does not marvel, under a full moon?" (*Hwa is on weorulde þæt ne wundrige fulles monan?*) As always, Shakespeare, too, helps us, when Count

Melun asks, "What in the world should make me now deceive?" in *King John*.

Now, *What the fuck is that?* is more au courant than *What the hell is that?* as *shit* and *fuck* have taken over the force that *damn* and *hell* have largely lost. The matron in *Glorifying the American Girl* would today say *shit*, not *damn*, having trouble getting more than two bars on her phone. In the same way, when *hell* was still hot pepper, one might spice up *What in the world…?* as *What in the hell…?* and indeed it started popping up in print in the 1700s.

However, in terms of how it's laid out, *What in the hell is that?* tickles a bit like a stray eyelash. We aren't referring to any hell, literal or figurative, that we are "in." The expression doesn't make sense anymore, and we process it as just a chunk: *wuddinthehell* is basically a naughty equivalent of *what*.

There are two things that can happen from there: you can lose the *in* or the *the*. Hence: *What in hell is that?* on the one hand, and on the other, our weird yet beloved *What the hell is that?* You retain the swagger from *hell*, but slimmed down since we've let go of *in*, which was meaningless anyway. The result— *hell* is no longer part of an ordinary prepositional phrase like *in the world* or *in the hell*. Instead, it's just part of an unmoored interjection *the hell*, crouching in the middle of the sentence, with its *the* hanging off. So:

STEP 1. What in the world is that?
STEP 2. What in the hell is that?
STEP 3. What the hell is that?

And after a while, the popularity of this expression created a tacit sense that *the hell* is a handy chunk to employ all over the place regardless of formal sense. Enter offshoot usages such as *the hell I will* and *ah, what the hell...* (i.e., is wrong with trying?) and remodeling the logical *to hell with it* into *the hell with it!* because we're so used to saying *the hell* in *What the hell is that?* In many ways yesterday's *goddamn* is today's *the hell*, a beefy, versatile shibboleth of unfettered colloquial English.

The fact remains: today most Anglophones only consider *damn* and *hell* profane in a formulaic sense. Colorful, perhaps. Unfit for children's ears, to be sure—or maybe they should only hear them a *little*. They are hardly the kind of words that leave you looking around to see if anyone else heard. In 1982, when I was in college, a peculiarly proper classmate of mine said *hell*, noticed a female student in the room, and said, "I'm sorry, I didn't know there was a lady present." To the rest of us this seemed about as unreachable as the nineteenth-century tradition of photographing deceased children propped up in chairs before their burial, and today our kids hear Ron in the Harry Potter movies erupting with *hell* all the time, with none of us blinking when the theme song for *Unbreakable Kimmy Schmidt* repeated *dammit* in its chorus.

Other words strike us as "real" profanity, and perhaps none more readily than one that begins with *f.*

2

WHAT IS IT ABOUT
FUCK?

In my schoolroom when I was about nine somebody scrawled *fuck* on a box.

It was on a box of cards of some pedagogical function I no longer recall. The person had carved the word into the soft cardboard with a pencil or perhaps a fingernail. *F U C K*, curving downward in the way that a preadolescent kid writes, all caps. Blunt, cocky, acrid, and sloppy—and the perpetrator likely barely knew what the word referred to. It was a stabby little yawp from the street corner desecrating the mellow, progressive atmosphere of a Montessori classroom in 1974. Or at least that's what it looked like to the teacher.

She made everybody sit silently until the culprit fessed up. It took about twenty minutes, an eternity for restless kids, before the guy who did it sniffingly came clean. There was high drama in all of this, of course, partly because, at least for me, it was my first encounter with the word. I was introduced to it as icily forbidden, even in that slightly bohemian atmosphere with the pink tower, the brown stairs, the chopping up of carrots as an "activity," and no homework.

I forget what happened to that kid—come to think of it, he wasn't back the following year, despite that his father was the principal's boyfriend. But what I retain from that weird afternoon late in the Nixon administration is that as enviably free as we were as schoolkids went, writing *fuck* crossed a line.

———

There is something about the word. In 1928, fabled Scribner editor Maxwell Perkins couldn't imagine uttering it even when discussing its usage in Ernest Hemingway's first draft of *A Farewell to Arms*; instead, he wrote it down on his desk calendar, tiptoeing around the word that, around that time, lexicographer Allen Walker Read described as "the word that has the deepest stigma of any in the language."

Fast-forward to ten years before that kid's prank in my classroom. In 1962, on *The Dick Van Dyke Show*, Ritchie Petrie writes that very word on a wall in school—of course, it's implied, never shown. His parents, Rob and Laura, are as horrified as Perkins would have been to find out the same thing about his own child four decades before, with Rob even quietly decreeing the word as "evil."

Between that episode and 2003, a lot happened in American culture, but after Bono yelled "This is fuckin' brilliant!" at the Golden Globes, the Federal Communications Commission (FCC) decreed it as "indecent and profane," as if we were still in Rob and Laura's black-and-white America, sleeping in separate beds. The FCC explored fining NBC and its affiliates for allowing the slur to air unbleeped, with the "eruption" discussed so widely that my failure to name-check it here would read as a yawning gap. Yet the FCC's condemnation came down in a nation in which, by then, no one was primly handing over *fuck* written on to-do slips to avoid speaking it aloud. The censure was both priggish and unsurprising—even seventy-five years after Perkins's post-Victorian watercooler diffidence, *fuck* still elicits a certain cowed genuflection.

What is it about *fuck*?

Origin Obscure

It tantalizes even in its origins, emerging quietly out of the mists of time. Among English's words, *fuck* is like that guest who arrives unseen but is seated with their drink by the time someone tings a glass to inaugurate the festivities.

English's vocabulary consists of two main layers. The starchier words tend to come from French and Latin, while the earthier ones are original English rootstock. The classic example involves meats. We use French words for the food Francophone noblemen under the Norman occupation savored at table, and English ones for the beasts that their Anglophone underlings had to kill to provide said victual delight. *Pork* is from French, *pig* is good old English; *beef* is French, *cow* is English. In fact, the fancy *victual* is from French—or more properly, French's daddy Latin. In French it had become *vitaille* (from which we later got the Western film sidekick's *vittles*) while the homely *food* is English.

English was for the lowdown, and this would lead one to suppose that *fuck*, referring to a mundane, essential business, would trace back through the centuries to an Old English word like *fuc* and that would be that—*picg* for "pig," *cu* for "cow," *fuc* for "fuck." The real story is trickier.

The earliest unequivocal use is an anonymous monk in 1528 whose annotations on a manuscript in Latin of a Cicero text on morals, *De Officiis*, include a weird parenthetical jag calling out a certain abbot—or, as the monk writes, a "fuckin abbott," complete with the missing *g*, redolent of our modern usage of *fuckin'*.

This scrawl neatly illuminates a fundamental shift in priorities regarding profanity at the time. In front of "fuckin abbott" is written "O d." One might assume this means "Old" and that the *l* wore away, but the space where an *l* would be is wide and clean. Rather, epigraphers reconstruct that the *d* is a coy abbreviation for *damned*, such that the full jape is "O, damned fuckin abbott." The takeaway is that in 1528, one euphemized the damned but not the fuckin', whereas today we would expect it to be the other way around, as it indeed would likely have been in a document like this a century or so later.

To wit, profanity first involved the holy, and only later the holes. The early Middle English speaker refrained from swearing to God and his progeny in vain, which included the recreational use of terms such as *damned*. Only starting in the 1400s, with the inward focus of the Reformation on personal uprightness as a demonstration of faith, as well as people spending more of their lives in private rather than communal spaces, did an unease with matters of sex and excretion come to the fore and eventually, with increasing secularism, relegate squeamishness about religious terms to the realm of archaism. Thus 1528's "O d fuckin abbott" could have been "O damned f abbott" by 1628.

For this monk to call someone a "fuckin'" anything lets us know that the basic sexual word *fuck* had long existed before. The monk was possibly using the term in a dismissive sense, as we might say "fuckin' taxes." If to fuck is considered lowly and often tacky, then naturally we will come to use the term for disparagement in general, unrelated to a sexual reference—just like how we might call someone who betrayed us a "little doublecrosser," even if they are six foot eight. Here, *little* has been extended to connote, again, dismissal: that which is not large easily lends itself to reinterpretation as "ethically small-minded." But that kind of extension takes time; you can only extend a word if it already exists. As such, where there is *fuckin'* there must already be *fuck*.

And there is clear evidence thereof, but for a long time, it's always at a certain distance, as if coyly hiding. For example, we can go a tad further back, to 1503, for a jolly usage of *fuck*—namely, *fukkit*, meaning "fucked"—but in Scots, not English. That was when poet William Dunbar ventured a bawdy stanza that seems only approximately comprehensible now, partly because even English itself was still Middle English, and Scots was something different again. The poem needs a bit of translation, therefore:

He clappit fast, he kist and chukkit,	He held fast, he kissed and fondled,
As with the glaikis he wer ouirgane;	As with the feeling he was overcome;
Yit be his feirris he wald have fukkit!	It seemed from his manner he would have fucked!
Ye brek my hart, my bony ane.	You break my heart, my bonny one.

One might sideline this as evidence only in a different language. Certainly, the past and present of the relationship between England and Scotland, and the speech varieties spoken in them respectively, make it a dicey issue whether we classify English and Scots as distinct tongues. The fact remains that a single population brought a language to an island in the

400s CE, which drifted into one rendition up north, now Scots, and a rendition southward that is now called English. Whether we call those renditions different languages or dialects of the same language is a judgment call upon which only politics and culture can decree. Assertions that Scots is not English must be respected.

However, this case straddles a line, and most would think of *fukkit* and *fucked* as twists on a single word. In the earlier stages of Middle English, the two were pronounced almost identically, with "fucked" pronounced as "FOOK-it." It also bears mentioning that just seven years after the "fuckin abbott" scrawl, a Scots play includes *fuck* with the spelling that we'd recognize, with a jape that "Bischops ... may fuck thair fill and be vnmaryit" (that is, unmarried).

Thus the Scots *fukkit* can qualify as a citation of *fuck*, alongside similar examples from around the same time. And *fuck* reveals itself even further back, in the 1400s—this time, literally, as the word is used in a code in which each letter is the one behind the actual letter. The poem, composed in 1475 in a kind of English-Latin hybrid, takes on certain friars of questionable chastity who "non sunt in coeli"—aren't in heaven—because they "gxddbov xxkxzt pg ifmk." What looks like gibberish actually means "they fuck wives of Ely."

Work out the *gxddbov* and you hit two obscurities. The *x* is for *u* despite our sense that *v* and *w* intervene between them because, first, *u* and *v* were considered the same—good Roman inscriptionese was JVLIVS Caesar and that sense of *u* took a while to fade. Then, *w* was written as "uu" and wasn't considered a separate business. So, *v* and *w* didn't yet exist, and hence before *x* came *u*. As such, at the end of *gxddbov*, if *u* and *v* are the same, then *v* is not *after* the *u* but *is* a *u*, which as always comes after *t*. If you take each letter one step back in the alphabet of the time, "gxddbov" emerges as *fuccant*—"they fuck"!

The coded *fuccant* is the earliest example we have of someone *expressing* our little word, but earlier than this are usages of *fuck* in personal names, vivid attestations that people certainly knew the word. Another century back, in 1310, Roger Fuckbythenavel is less of a surprise than he may have been otherwise. He is listed in court records, and whether that qualified as a surname or nickname for being a scamp is less the issue than that it was used at all. And Roger wasn't alone. A few decades before, in the late 1200s, we find ordinary citizens such as Henry Fuckbeggar and Simon Fuckbutter, and not as scrawls in privy stalls: Mr. Fuckbeggar was in Edward I's retinue. This was an England in which one could take a stroll down Gropecunt Lane reminiscing fondly about lunches al fresco in Fuckinggrove. One of the things that would most throw us as time travelers to the Middle Ages would be how casually people of all strata used words for sex, excretion, and the body parts involved. Again, in this era one talked nervously around matters of God—what was up there, not down there.

Fuckbeggar did have an alternate name, *Bute-vilein*, meaning "hit-churl," as in "churl-hitter" in the same way as a pickpocket is someone who picks a pocket—here, someone who would hit a humble guy. But the explanation strains for Fuckbythenavel. Sure, of late one may refer to "hitting that" as a way of referring to the conjugal act. But when it's about the belly button, and what it sits directly north of, isn't our meaning of *fuck* both more likely and more representative of the wit that undergirds the human spirit?

Mr. Fuckbutter was indeed a dairyman, but while we might think of butter churning as a kind of hitting, let's face it, the physical parallel with you-know-what is rather precise. Not only that, at the time these names were committed to paper, we also find our first attestations of the bird called a *windfucker*. More interesting is that windfuckers are the kind of bird that *mount* the wind and sail upon it.

What about John the Fucker, who *technically* gives us our very first *fuck*, in 1278? Well, he was John *le* Fucker, and the French angle puts him out of the running. His name resembled our *fuck* only accidentally, being but one of many possible outcomes of a common French name of the period that started as Fulchier and Fulker; there were Fulchers as far back as Old English before the Norman conquest.

Repeat words like *Fulchier* and *Fulker* over long enough a period, and chances are the *l* is going to wear away. Just as the word *soldier* was pronounced "so-jure" by Fucker John's time, and today *solder* is pronounced "SAH-der," Fulchier often became Fucher. Or even Fuker, given that in French of the period, words often existed in versions with *ch* and versions with a *k* sound: usually *k* for Normans and *ch* for Parisians. Our *castle*, for example, is from Norman; *château* is the same word with the Parisian *ch*. *Château* is to *castle* as *Fulcher* is to *Fucker*.

Regardless, if people were hearing it as "Fucker," then all of this business about French sounds might qualify as inside baseball. But actually, the Fucker here would have been pronounced in the 1200s as "foo-CARE." (Today, we'd write it Le Foucaire—very Clouseauesque.) In an oral culture where names were heard rather than written except when occasionally scribed on paper for some official reason, Le Foucaire would not have sounded like "fucker" at all. It reminds me of the Britcom *Keeping Up Appearances*, in which snotty matron Hyacinth insists on disguising her husband's humble surname Bucket by insisting on pronouncing it "Boo-KAY."

Thus "Ye olde Fucker John" is too good to be true. However, his contemporaries Messrs. Fuckbythenavel and Fuckbutter document that our word was alive and well in medieval English. But when we go back further we hit a wall.

Anglo-Sexin'?

Middle English's *fuck* should trace back to a Beowulfian verb like *fucan*, but in all the Old English prose and poetry that we have, there is no such word. The closest is *fician*, which if it had come down to modern English would be "fike." This meant to deceive, as in to "fike" someone. It has a certain *fuck* flavor, to be sure, in that we today can use *fuck* to mean to screw someone over. But that meaning grows *from* the sexual one—for better or for worse, one can extend the power relation implied by *fuck* to, metaphorically, overpowering a person and thus, selling them short.

The problem is that Old English only offers what looks like that second-stage extension—*fikeing someone over*—not the root meaning about sex. Did the word begin meaning "deceive" and then come to mean "to have sex with"? Not likely. This would suggest a rather cynical and even unconfident take on one's skills. To wit, it had to go from fucking to fucking over, not the reverse. Plus, the vowel is wrong—how did we get from *fick* to *fuck*?

A certain scholarly consensus has coalesced on German— from which English has borrowed many words—in which *ficken* once could mean to rub. This *ficken* word is part of a linguistic family in which a pattern of sounds tends to indicate a general meaning. This happens in all languages: just as English words beginning with *gl-* often refer to light twinkling—*glimmer*, *glint*, *glow*—and words beginning with *sl-* often refer to icky snakish movement—*slink*, *slither*, *slime*—in German dialects, words sounding like *fick* hover around a concept that starts with rubbing and extends from there.

Fickeln can mean to play a violin. To run around back and

forth is to *fickfack*, and a crowd doing that is a *Gefick*. *Fick* basically meant, it would seem, to move quickly back and forth. This means that a slang term for penis has been *Fickel*, and that we settle upon the essence of the matter in that dialectal German for *fuck* actually is *ficken*. I recall, from my youthier days, someone warning me against meeting with a woman I knew in Germany, saying that she merely wanted what is called a "Qvikfick" (in that case, inaccurately [alas?]).

But: just as with English's *fick*, the vowel is wrong. If English took it from German, then why don't we today call people motherfickers? We get *blitz* from German, and have not transformed it into "blutz." If we look at similar German words containing a *u*, then we drift too far afield. *Fucken* is to hurry; *fuckeln* is to scratch—close, but most would say no cigar. *Fucksen* is to treat ill—which would again seem a self-hating origin. And with *Fucker* meaning "bellows," most of us will surrender.

None of it quite hits the mark. We also have to ask why English speakers would have borrowed a term for sex from their German drinking buddies—all of us, eventually. Many English speakers know, for example, that German for *shit* is *Scheisse*. American soldiers in World War I were given to calling the Kaiser the "Shiser," as one sees in a cartoon scrawled on a letter a police officer in New York wrote at the armistice. Or you may recall the *South Park* episode referring to a pornographic German "Scheisse video," broadcast with the assumption that most viewers would be familiar with the word. Yet none of us are likely to *replace* our own words for *poop* with *Scheisse*. If a language has plenty of its own words for something, it's unlikely to take one from some other language, much less let it all but choke out all the others.

Of course, stranger things have happened. However, the larger picture makes it even more unlikely. In general, the idea that *fuck* came from German runs up against that neither Old nor Middle English speakers are known to have sampled German (Low or other) for loan words in any defining, chapter-worthy way. No book on the history of English even includes a chapter on German borrowings, as opposed to ones from Scandinavian, French, and Latin.

That is, the reason rural Brits have been known to refer to planting seed as "fucking the field" is not because of a word adopted from invaders or immigrants to the island, but something more immediate. Two possibilities beckon.

One is that *fuck* does trace back to Old English and no evidence of it happens to have survived. It wasn't hard to be an Old English word and get lost to the ages. Only about 34,000 Old English words are known to us, compared to the 225,000 modern English ones in that medium-size dictionary you may have taken to college. Add to this that most Old English writing centered on a rather narrow range of topics mostly official and elegiac, and we can see how shaky it is to assume Old English lacked a word simply because we don't know it today. (Imagine future linguists deciding that twenty-first-century

English had no word *fuck* simply because it didn't appear in *Charlotte's Web*, an episode of *Good Times*, and five issues of the *New Yorker*.)

I would bet not all of my money, but a good bit of it, that if you stood in a town square somewhere in Northumbria in 600 CE and yelled out *Uton fucan!*—"Let's fuck!"—heads would turn, some pearl-clutchingly appalled and others naughtily amused, and likely more the latter. They'd have known the word and its meaning, and the literate among them would have been baffled that anyone would ever write it in a book.

One indication in support is that *fuck* isn't the only word in Middle English that seems like it would have begun as Old English's *fucan*. There is a whole family of what seems like its spawn, such as *fudge*, which can mean "to thrust in awkwardly or irrelevantly." Again, we wonder about self-regard, but in terms of both the sound and the meaning, this would be a more plausible descendant from *fucan* than "fike" meaning "fib." *Fadge* in some regions of Britain has meant to make one's way, and *fidge*, or *fitch*, has meant to touch something a lot. It is hardly implausible that these words are the progeny of the original, by chance never making it into solemnly scribed documents about wars, regal succession, and governance, but of which one child, *fuc(k)*, fell especially close to the tree, preserved the straight-up reference to sexing, and was used on Middle English–speaking streets unrecorded except in some bawdy surnames.

But just as likely is that *fuck* started in another language altogether, that of the Vikings that began invading England in 787 AD. Marrying English women and having children with them, they were in a perfect position to lend their own words to the language they were learning, and especially one referring to something they were doing often. Indeed hundreds of everyday words like *happy*, *get*, and *skirt* started in the language that would soon become Danish, Swedish, and Norwegian. A now obsolete Norwegian word like *fukka* would have been a fine candidate for what became our four-letter word of choice. This time, no squinting is necessary—*fukka* meant exactly what it looks like. The Scandinavian account also explains that efflorescence of *fukkit* and the like in earlier Scots; for reasons connected to where the Vikings landed and settled most densely, Viking-inflected English was possibly a more robust contributor to Scots language than it was to what became standard English.

We will likely never be absolutely sure which of these origin stories is the right one. And of course both may be right. Most Old English words are long gone, replaced by Norse, French, and Latin ones. It would have helped *fucan* to hold on if the Vikings had their own word with the same sound and meaning that matched it. Overall, however, our word shall likely ever remain the mysterious little *fuck* that it is, turning up off in a corner of the lexical firmament sometime after the Battle of Hastings.

Hiding in Plain Sight

The fossil record turns peculiar again, though. After its thirteenth-century premiere, the word builds gradually, crests—and then for just as long again, dwindles into shards and hints. The "fuckin abbott" note isn't the only time the word appears in the 1500s, but—just as backward in time we see ever fewer cases until we are forced into rummaging around in Norwegian—after the 1500s there are ever fewer *fuck*s in print and then all but none.

In the 1500s and before, it was, to be sure, naughty. The coded *fuccant* in 1475 is pure Beavis and Butthead, and there's no way Fuckbythenavel was a name gravely passed on from fathers to sons by candlelight as Mrs. Fuckbythenavel lay with her new babe in arms. However, *fuck* was tolerated—on no level did one pretend it didn't exist. From the Renaissance on, however, *fuck* becomes less salty than profane.

With some dirty words, we let assorted double entendres pass in daily life. There are countless fellows in no need of therapy who spend their lives nicknamed Dick. I went to college with a guy whose last name was Fellus, and from what I could tell, it concerned him not at all, and even didn't prevent him from capturing the heart of the stunning English redhead who lived in the dorm room next to mine. Yet she wouldn't have given him the time of day if his last name were Fucker—despite that her ancestors had been taking the arm of guys with names like Fuckbutter.

Rather, since the Renaissance, *fuck* has been the subject of a grand cover-up, the lexical equivalent of the drunken uncle or the pornography collection, under which a word known well and even adored by most is barred from public presentation. After the 1500s, *fuck* is rarely printed except, again, in code or elision, and eventually appears in no dictionary from 1795 to 1965—that is, from the dawn of the American nation to Bob Dylan playing electric guitar. One imagines those future lexicographers decreeing that *fuck* for some reason came, shone, and then vanished from this earth, like brachiopods and *Bosom Buddies*. Yet there are endless indications that the word was thriving and even exploding in real life despite its near-absence in print.

We will recall Babe Ruth's father's bartender who attested on paper that he "fucked Mrs Geo. H, Ruth March 12 1906." Working-class Baltimoreans during the aughts, it would seem, knew the word as closely as we do. But only under wraps. Eighteen years later, in 1924, the play *What Price Glory* about US soldiers in World War I was renowned for its profanity, with viewers of the silent film version two years later challenged to try to read the actors' lips. Yet the script for this play, supposedly so nakedly foul-mouthed, included nary a *fuck* (or *shit*).

Crucially, however, British soldiers were described around

the same time, 1930, as using *fuck* with a fecundity that feels utterly modern:

> *It became so common that an effective way for the soldier to express this emotion was to omit this word. Thus if a sergeant said "Get your —ing rifles!" it was understood as a matter of routine. But if he said "Get your rifles!" there was an immediate implication of urgency and danger.*

And, of course, even this chronicler had to use dashes. Later, the term *snafu* began as a soldier's acronym in World War II for "situation normal: all fucked up."

Norman Mailer's soldiers in *The Naked and the Dead* famously said *fug*, and his readers knew exactly what he meant. In the 1957 musical *West Side Story*, the street toughs couldn't be heard using the word the way their real-life equivalents did, but lyricist Stephen Sondheim conveyed its flavor with "buggin'"—the Jets want to best "Every last buggin' gang on the whole buggin' street"—and we certainly know what "Gee, Officer Krupke, krup you!" refers to.

Nor was *fuck* only used in menacing and hypermasculinized contexts. Hemingway wrote letters that said things like "They have sent me a wrapper—admirably conceived—beautifully executed (fuck this typewriter) for the 5th printing)." That was in reference to a new cover for *The Sun Also Rises*, in which men's men, drinking, fighting, and competing, never say *fuck*—even macho Hem had to knuckle under the reigning piety, of the kind that had his editor, Max Perkins, scribbling nervously on his calendar. By 1940, Hemingway had more clout, but still the best he could manage was to festoon *For Whom the Bell Tolls* with *mucks*: "Oh, muck my grandfather and muck this whole treacherous muckfaced country and every mucking Spaniard in it on either side and to hell forever."

Long before Lenny Bruce and George Carlin, the word was everywhere, peeking from behind its veil. *What Price Glory* isn't the only silent film that merits lip-reading; in 1927's *Hula*, screen siren Clara Bow clearly says "Fuck" during a scene in a lake. Smutty underground comic books of the 1930s yield another look. "Lady—I'm the fuckinest slob that ever sailed the seven seas," says Popeye, and I'll spare you what came after that (except that someone asks Wimpy to "fuck me ragged"). Harold Teen was a proto–Archie Andrews, which should give you a sense of how faceless and vanilla he was, and even he asserts, "When I wanna fuck I'm gonna *fuck*!" You can probably imagine how these "comix" dealt with Archie himself and Betty and Veronica.

The comic strip characters' usage suggests that we would only expect its open airing by the dismissible, the silly, those not to be taken seriously. This may explain an especially weird and resonant usage in *Bosko's Picture Show* of 1933, in which the first Looney Tunes character, Bosko, a Mickey Mouse knockoff of vaguely Black American affect, calls a villain "the dirty fuck!" There are claims that Bosko actually said "mug" or "fox," but *fuck* is crystal clear on the soundtrack, as is Bosko's mouth shape for *f*—and the interloper doesn't seem to be a fox. It seems to have had something to do with the fact that this was the last cartoon for the studio by these creators, who slipped it in as a nose-thumbing to the irritating producer. (His name was Leon Schlesinger, and he had a way of getting under people's skin and, apparently, even for eliciting that word. Legendary animator Shamus Culhane was hired briefly by the studio in the early forties with the promise that he was being groomed to direct his own cartoons. Upon finding out that this was not in the cards, he resigned, telling Schlesinger to "perform an impossible sexual act"—or at least, that's how Culhane, as a man of his times, felt moved to describe it decades later.)

Anecdotes like that make us want to hear people (not Bosko) back then *saying* it, and we can, but not in movies or on old radio. Blues songs were, in their way, a kind of comic strip, and in them, Black Americans, especially, could hear *fuck* used after-hours. We know this because of an especially piquant 1935 recording by Lucille Bogan, often celebrated as third to Black blues queens Ma Rainey and Bessie Smith, that got around clandestinely as a "party record":

Say, I fucked all night and all dem nights before, baby,
And I feel jus' like I wanna fuck some mo'
Oh, Great God, Daddy, grind me honey, shave me dry!

and:

Now fuckin' was a thing that would take me to heaven
I'll be fuckin' in the studio till the clock strikes eleven
Aw, Daddy, Daddy, shave 'em dry.
I'll fuck you, baby—honey, I'll make you cry!

Otherwise, though, the taboo nature of the word was a spark for wit of a finer brand. In Ernst Lubitsch's classic 1942 film *To Be or Not to Be*, a Nazi colonel opines, in one of the surest laugh lines, "Oh, yes, I saw him in *Hamlet* once. What he did to Shakespeare we are doing now to Poland!" Dorothy Parker wrote theater reviews early in her career, which were just as funny as anything she wrote or said later, and in 1922 included a comment on one justly forgotten trifle: "If I were to tell you the plot of the piece, in detail, you would feel that the only honorable thing for you to do would be to marry me."

Why the pox on a word so many people were using and that referred simply to sex? Tiptoeing around it seems ordinary to us now, but recall that medievals used it freely—maybe with a giggle, but accepting it as reflecting a staple of human life. Yet our culture only started loosening up on it after World War II, as Victorian mores drifted ever further into the past, and American, British, and other Anglophone populaces had become more cosmopolitan as the result of the military experience and more widespread access to education. Even here, change was slow. In 1951, Scribner allowed a few dozen *fuck*s in James Jones's war novel *From Here to Eternity*, but this was considered a big deal, the 1953 film retained no hint of such language, and the book was banned from the mails in 1955. The dam only broke after the *Lady Chatterley's Lover* obscenity trial in 1960. But, still, the Bono kerfuffle occurred in the twenty-first century.

Keeping It Fresh

By 1939, Rhett Butler could say *damn* but not *fuck*, because of the shift from cursing about your Jesus to cursing about your junk.

Then there is likely the *sound* of the word. Few could pretend there isn't a certain satisfaction in the sheer utterance of *fuck* beyond that you get from saying *damn* or *shit*. As linguist and cognitive scientist Benjamin Bergen has taught us, profanity in English tends to consist of words of one syllable ending with a consonant. *Fuck* has that down—but then, *fuck* beat out similarly equipped competitors. Middle English also had *sard*, *dight*, and *swive* with the same meaning. *Swive* was especially interesting: *dribble* means to drip repeatedly within a short period of time, *nibble* means to nip repeatedly within a short period of time, *prickle* means to prick repeatedly within a short period of time, and *swivel* means to... get it?

But *swive* and the gang all fell away, and we are likely back to sheer sound. Just as *sl-* sounds like slithering, *f* and *k* linked by a hearty vowel not only perhaps sound more like the action in question than do *swive*, *sard*, or *dight*, but are more fun to spit out. The similarly shaped German words for *penises* and maybe even *bellows* attests to this judgment. (It's hard to imagine Stanley Kubrick closing *Eyes Wide Shut* with Nicole Kidman saying "Sard.")

Too, *fuck* harbors a certain power because of its contribution to an ever-churning refreshment of the piquant. *Damn* and *hell* were once strong brew, enough to render *What Price Glory* seriously scandalous, enough so that Ernest Hemingway's mother, a woman of the world champing at the bits of traditionalism in her time, cringed to see such words in her son's work. But once *fuck* was freed from its shackles after the 1960s, we found it useful as a reset for the aging, and thus less potent, nature of older curses.

"What the hell?" one might say during World War II, as Jackie Gleason did, repeatedly, in Broadway's *Follow the Girls* when surprised or disrespected, which was celebrated as a highlight of the show. But a couple of decades later "What the *fuck*" was the locution of choice. These days, even that is getting a little old, which is why "What the shit?" is creeping in to freshen things up once again. On the flip side, whereas in the old days one gave a shit or did not, after the 1960s one increasingly gave not a shit but a fuck. "Damn that" is very old-school to us only because "Fuck that" set in as a replacement after those good old 1960s.

In Hollywood blooper reels of the 1930s and 1940s, when actors mess up they say "damn" and "son of a bitch" but never, from what I have seen, "fuck," which the actors in *Will & Grace* and *Breaking Bad* shout when blowing a line. And despite how hot the cussing supposedly was in the silent *What Price Glory*, a lip-reading yields only *son of a bitch* and maybe *prick*. In 1938, the animators of Looney Tunes did a stag reel for a party in which Porky Pig hit his thumb with a hammer repeatedly and kept stuttering "Son of a bi—, son of a bi—, son of a bi— gun!" only to finally say, "You thought I was gonna say son of a *bitch*, didn't ya?" Okay, but the more likely reaction today would be *Fuck!*

That's what I would, most definitely, say, while I'm pretty sure my father would have said "Shit!" My parents were reserved persons who nevertheless liked their "nip" on a weekend night, after which they were often given, like Louis Armstrong's wife, to assorted degrees of honest expression. I recall them, in the 1970s and 1980s, indulging in a good deal of savory and articulate *damn*, *hell*, and *shit*, but reserving *fuck* for the extreme and rarely uttering it around me and my sister until we were teenagers. I am also a rather reserved person, but I nevertheless use *fuck* casually in a way that would have disqualified me from any drawing rooms just a few decades ago. *Fuck* is fresh.

Multi-fucking-farious

Fuck is as fertile as it is fresh, as if bearing out its connotation.

In some circles, the sheer frequency with which one can say it is dazzling. Most of us are familiar with its usage almost as punctuation in the casual speech of, especially, male teens and twentysomethings, especially since the late 1970s. Sociolinguist William Labov did extensive recordings of Black young men in rough neighborhoods in the 1960s, and while they were as comfortable with profanity as one would expect, they did not use *fuck* with anything like the frequency that newer generations do today. The word had yet to fully oust *damn* and *hell*.

Actress and singer Elaine Stritch, born in 1925, said late in her life, "I don't want to get drunk. I don't want to cause trouble. I don't want to say fuck. I don't want to make any more sacrifices. I just want to have a drink a day. Anybody buying?" Note the implication—*fuck* was a big deal in line with causing trouble, and more likely after the sun goes down and when under the influence. Compare to John Goodman's character on David Simon's *Treme* series hauling off with "Fuck you, you fuckin' fucks!" sober and in broad daylight.

That last sentence also exemplifies the wild variety of meanings we can take from *fuck*. Consider: the word *foot* began, in the father language to most of Europe's languages, as *ped*. That word developed into not only *foot*, but *fetter*, *fetch*, *impediment*, *impeach*, *pajamas*, *pessimism*, *impeccable*, *pioneer*, *octopus*, and *peccadillo*. One might glow a bit to learn such a thing, and *fuck* is awesome in the same way. Imagine someone brand-new to English asking:

NEWBIE: *What means this "fuck"?*

Us: *It means having sex!*

NEWBIE: *But you all use it a lot more. Sometimes I can't understand what you mean!*

Us: *You mean, like, "What the fuck?"*

NEWBIE: *Yes, yes, that "What the fuck," "fucking" that, "the fuck" this—what is this? You are always fucking what?*

Us: *Oh, well, it's when you're . . . emphasizing something. Like . . . (heh) "Fuck you!"* (ACCOMPANIED BY A VIGOROUS HAND GESTURE)

Intuitively we might call it emphasis, since our feeling while uttering it is often emphatic. But are we not selling the person short in saying that emphasis is what fuck "means"? That doesn't work for *Fuck you!* In *I don't have any fucks left to give*, too, the fucks in question are not matters of emphasis. If anything, one is conveying a lack of concern, which entails downplaying rather than adding significance. Consider:

Fuck you!
Oh well, fuck that.
What the fuck?
What the fuck is . . .
Get the fuck out of here.
You fuck.
You dumb/sick/stupid fuck.

I don't give a fuck.
That's fucking brilliant.
Get your fucking hands off me.
He fucked him over.
He got fucked in the deal.
You fucked up.
Fuck!

That list (1) is incomplete and (2) clearly demonstrates that we're talking about more than just "emphasis." Beyond sex, *fuck* can connote so very much more: destruction (*fuck it up*), deception (*fucked me over*), dismissal (*Fuck it!*), daunting (*Get your fucking hands off!*) and the down-to-earth. The latter happens in cases such as praising someone by saying, as I once heard someone do, "He helped build the fuckin' space shuttle!" The connotation is that participating in that project renders his intelligence a solid truth of the kind we all agree upon, a barstool verity rather than a proposition up for exploration: "Come on, let's face it, there's no use talkin'... "—this fact is as simple and true as fucking. The word is, indeed, that loaded.

In fact, if English were left to morph along with no one complaining that new developments were "bad grammar," then *fuck* would be well on its way to becoming a question word. In rapid speech, *What the fuck is that?* can become *Fuck's that?* Think also of *Fuck are you talkin' about?* Imagine being a foreigner learning English by ear—they'd hear those sentences more often than their complete versions (perhaps they're for some reason on a year abroad restricted to the set of *Mean Streets* or *The Wire*). They could logically assume that *fuck* means *what*, such that the textbook *What is that?* would be, in this English 2.0, *Fuck is that?*

Instead, though, we can be satisfied with *fucking* insertion. Or, to use a fancier term, expletive infixation. Many will recall Eliza Doolittle's "abso-blooming-lutely" but might not relate it to an American usage such as Cinci-fucking-nati. The joy of *fucking* insertion is that it requires understanding a subtle rule, and thus qualifies as grammatical competence just as much as knowing to say *I'm turning nineteen tomorrow* rather than *I will turn nineteen tomorrow*. Note: Phila-fucking-delphia, but not Al-fucking-toona. Cinci-fucking-nati, but not Cin-fucking-cinnati and certainly not Cincinna-fucking-ti.

The rule is that the *fucking* has to sit between two accented units. That means that you can say fan-fucking-tastic because one so often says *fantastic* with a jolly accent on the *fan-* part. However, no one would be described as ar-fucking-tistic (there's no accent on the *ar*), nor would we spend the winter in Mi-fucking-ami. Then, Bos-fucking-ton doesn't work because there's no accent on the *-ton*. Rather, if there aren't two accented syllables to slip between, the *fucking* has to just come before—hence fuckin' Miami and fuckin' Boston despite Colo-fucking-rado and Massa-fucking-chusetts.

———

As we take our leave from *fuck*, I can't help mentioning that on ye olde Fucker John and the descent of his surname from an antique French name Fulcher, I refrained from mentioning one of the chance renditions of the original word. One outcome of Fulcher, as humans rolled it around in their mouths over the generations, was Folger. Those of us who remember television's Mrs. Olson, as well as those of us who are in on the fact that instant coffee is actually somewhat better than one might think despite the cultural penetration of Starbucks, can enjoy that on a certain abstract level, there are people across America starting their day with a good hot cup of Fucker's Coffee.

* 3 *

PROFANITY
AND SHIT

Our culture's pox on bodily matters can look downright bizarre in its earlier manifestations. In the film *42nd Street* in 1933, two showgirls hunched in a train berth in their pajamas sing a stanza from the song in progress, "Shuffle Off to Buffalo":

He did right by little Nellie
With a shotgun at his bel… tummy
How could he say no?
He just had to shuffle
Shuffle off to Buffalo.

It's Ginger Rogers singing, in fact, about three seconds before becoming iconic as half of Fred and Ginger. But why does this showgirl, a salty and experienced gal, in the era in which movie characters were freely saying *damn* and *hell*, stop herself saying *belly* and substitute *tummy*?

Because of a post-Victorian sense that it was vulgar to refer directly to the stomach because of what it was just above! Better to use a baby word like *tummy*. It's a neat moment: sentiments about taking the Lord's name in vain were falling away, yet those regarding the body were still influential enough to restrain these "chippies."

In a short comedy around the same time, originally silent comedian Charley Chase—think a silent film version of Dick Van Dyke—has a coy exchange with a young woman where they simper and hesitate when referring to a garment known as a stomacher, again baffling us now. But here was an era in which a bourgeois sense still reigned that one at least pretended to avoid summoning thoughts of "down there," regarding either what one did with it or what emerged therefrom.

Feces, then, was disallowed from respectable discussion; *shit* was completely profane. For all the ballyhoo about the frankness of early talkies, those characters might venture *damn* and *hell*, but there isn't a *shit* in any of them. The closest occurred the year before *42nd Street*, and stuns exactly because the ban was otherwise so strict in popular culture.

In the comedy-drama *Prosperity*, the grand old comic actress Marie Dressler plays a woman of a certain age, who, for reasons that need not detain us, accidentally ingests a good deal of a laxative. For the fade-out joke at the end, she makes a rousing speech on her balcony to assembled townspeople, wrapping up the plot, flashes a bit of a grimace and says, "And now, if you'll excuse me!" and hastily goes back inside, clearly to attend to, ahem, pressing matters.

One marvels that this got by Hollywood censors even before the Code. After, popular culture restricted discussion of "number one" to oblique references regarding babies and dogs, while "number two" might as well not have existed.

But profanity cannot be silenced; profanity wants to get busy. As with the other words we have visited, *shit* has permeated the English language far beyond reference to feces or a way to express anger. It can be a noun, pronoun, verb, or adjective; with a bit of adjustment it can be an adverb; it can convey celebration or vagueness, dismissal or nullity—quite the journey for a word that means "poop."

From the Bowels of History

Some will tell you that the journey started belowdecks. One deathless tale has it that *shit* started as an acronym—*ship high in transit*—supposedly marked on bags of manure when transported by sea in some unspecified earlier era. This time differed from ours in that certain locales apparently needed to have dung imported, and the issue was keeping the manure dry. If it was packed down deep in the hull, then got wet, decomposition created methane gas, which, if meeting the lantern of an unwary sailor sneaking down at night to get a peek at the shitbags, could blow the boat to pieces.

This story neglects how far back words tend to go, and it's easy to disprove. *Shit* is alive and well in Old English, before 1000 CE, long before a sentence like "ship high in transit" would even have been possible, because among other things, *transit* had yet to enter the language. Then also, *shit* is one kitten in a litter of equivalent words in other Germanic languages, like it in shape and meaning. That is, some single word in an ancestor tongue, spoken around twenty-five hundred years ago around what would become Denmark, before English existed, birthed descendants all over northern and western Europe: *schijt* in Dutch; *skit* in Swedish; *Scheisse* in German. In those languages, the acronym "ship high in transit" would look nothing like *s-h-i-t*.

Perhaps they took on *shit* the way English later took on *sushi*? It seems doubtful. All the words, including ours, emerged long before there even existed English sailors, much less one warning his mates about exploding bags of manure. Equally doubtful is that those hypothetical sailors would start using such an acronym. Presumably they, too, already had a name for the stuff.

And finally we must revisit the question: Who would have

been seeking and purchasing bags of crap by the bushel and why? Yes, in the nineteenth century, guano boats furnished western Europe and the United States with bird and bat poop from South America, uniquely nutrient-rich and handy as fertilizer, for a spell. But this was long, long after we have solid evidence that the word *shit* had already existed essentially forever.

The real origin story has its charms, although a less dramatic one than the one about shit boats. English ultimately traces back to a language spoken by people living in what is now Ukraine, who almost certainly used a word *skei* that meant "cut off" or "slice." Over the millennia, some of their descendants settled in England, with *skei* having morphed to *scit*. But in Old English, its meaning had drifted into a particular kind of cutting off. Likely some people along the way started referring to defecation as going to "cut one off" or the like—the expression *to pinch a loaf* is unavoidable as a comparison. *Sc-* soon became *sh-*, and so just as a *scip* was our *ship*, *scit* is, um, yeah.

Talk about six degrees—you never know which words will be related, both within and between languages. The ancient *skei* spread to hundreds of languages both westward in Europe and eastward into Asia, emerging with different shapes and meanings in all of them. In Greek, *skei* transformed in ways that make sense to us as variants on "cut off," such as *schism* and *schizoid* that refer to division, that which has been cut asunder.

Latin was more creative: *skei* became *sci*—or, with the verbal ending that had emerged in it, *scire*, a word you might recognize from high school Latin as simply the respectable word for "to know."

Careful study shows that this, too, was related to the original meaning. The idea was that to know is to slice matters, make careful distinctions, the way philosophers such as Plato and Aristotle so exhaustively laid out their assumptions when attempting an argument. President Andrew Johnson of all people once laid out this classical sense of "knowing" beautifully, saying that he wished he had become a scholar because "it would have satisfied my desire to analyze things, to examine them in separate periods and then unite them again to view them as a whole."

English inherited *scire* by borrowing from Latin in the word *science*. This means that *shit* and *science* are brother words despite their starkly opposite demeanors. *Conscience*, too, as a combination of *con* "with" and *science*, is a sibling of a word that in English means "feces." Or, in my favorite example, *nice* traces back to Latin *nescius*, as in *ne* "not" and *scius* being a form of our friend *scire* and meaning "knowing." The way words alter and pivot through time never fails to astonish me—remember, *hell* starts as hades and ends up meaning *even*; to us, *nice* means "blandly pleasing" but *nescius* meant "ignorant." Here's the genealogy: if you're ignorant you're weak; if you're weak you're fussy; if you're fussy you're dainty; if you're dainty you're precise and proper; if you're precise and proper you are rated as agreeable. At least this is how English evolved over almost a thousand years as *nice* went from dum-dum to your dependably inoffensive cousin Roberta. But this means that *shit* and *nice* were once related as closely as the Winklevoss brothers are depicted in *The Social Network*. Think of *nescius* meaning "not shit," and you pretty much get *nice*.

Plowed Under

In Old and Middle English, *shit* was used as freely as *poop* is today. It seemed absurd, when most people lived on the land, to be coy about something one's animals did daily, and that one did oneself about as frequently, and with less privacy than people would later. Ancient and medieval English speakers felt about *shit* roughly the way American Anglophones now feel about *damn*—roughly, "What's the big deal?"

The sea change from the free writing of "shitte" to the word not appearing in the *Webster's New World Dictionary* as late as 1970 began after the Reformation. Protestantism stressed an inwardly focused quest to demonstrate one's faith in Jesus via the avoidance of sin. To the extent that the body itself was classified as waywardly inclined, as an undependable "flesh" resisting the discipline of the mind, words and expressions suggesting transgression acquired a new sense of threat.

Then also, from the sixteenth century on in England, people experienced ever greater degrees of what we know as privacy. Mercantile prosperity, plus innovations in heating technology, allowed many bigger houses with more rooms. This encouraged a sense that certain things were private rather than public matters. As late as the 1400s, the nobleman feeling the call of nature would take care of his needs off in a corner of the stairwell. He wouldn't take his daughter on his shoulders to watch him do it, nor did anyone normally chat him up while he was in the act, but the private privy, the private bedroom, the eclipse of times when all saw one another naked on a regular basis and children were accustomed to listening to and even watching their parents have sex, all reinforced a sense that bodily matters were to be kept to yourself. Religious convictions as well as architectural innovations now made possible this reticence.

Anthropology teaches us that there are no human societies in which feces is not considered repulsive, so it is predictable that starting in the 1500s, *shit* would be classified as profane in the sense of *damn* and *hell*. In the 1630s, the Latin term *feces* crept in as a polite alternative (*excrement* first referring to any old substance seeping out of the body). We see the artfully euphemistic nature of *feces* in its Latin meaning of "dregs," like those of wine at the bottom of a barrel full of it. That rather deftly nails things without getting too specific.

Shit was from then on a "bad" word, and that evaluation carried over the Atlantic. In the early twentieth century, Edna St. Vincent Millay and her sister were bedazzled by the atmosphere of Greenwich Village, where, as *The Masses* cartoonist Art Young described, a woman could say *damn* without being looked at askance. Edna's sister late in her life recalled, "So we sat darning socks on Waverly Place and practiced the use of profanity as we stitched. Needle in, shit. Needle out, piss. Needle in, fuck. Needle out, cunt." This teaches us that in some contexts ordinary people were using the word *shit* all the time. But we can only know it now by eavesdropping, such as perusing their graffiti. Lexicographer Allen Walker Read did just this in the late 1920s, uncovering latrine poetry such as the flinty "Roses are red, violets are blue, I took a shit, and so did you," or this one of 1928 from the Yellowstone Park campground, delicately straddling the tautological and the haikuesque:

This Shithouse stinks like shit
Because it is so shitty

And by 1928, we reach the era of early talkie films, which are invaluable in lending us a sense of how Americans processed profanity between the wars, at a time now a century in the past. When was the first time someone said *shit* on film? Goodness, how much fun it would be if that same Charley Chase who was so dainty about "stomacher" actually did say "shitty" somewhere—and it seems like it, in 1930's *All Teed Up*, which is about golf. A weird moment at the end is when Chase, frustrated, breaks some golf clubs and seems to yell, "You can take these shitty sticks . . . !" But alas, if you play it again and again you realize he was saying "shinny sticks," a term for hockey sticks.

I'd bet quite a lot that the first *shit* on film was made the year before at that same Hal Roach studio, an early Laurel and Hardy romp. But it's an accident we aren't supposed to catch. In 1929, with sound having come to film only a year or two before, actors trained in silents were still getting used to the fact that anything they said would be recorded and heard. As character actor Edgar Kennedy plays his usual frustrated melonhead, now trying to get out of a crowded car, he unmistakably grunts under his breath, "Oh, shit!"

Then, I venture that the first *shit* on a musical recording was in 1935. Lucille Bogan's underground recording, which I mentioned in the previous chapter, includes a moment that sounds like she is reading the lyric for the first time—this being likely a one-off prank that would not be officially released—and after she sings the likes of (get ready!):

Now your nuts hang down like a damned bell clapper
And your dick stands up like a steeple.
Your goddamned asshole stands open like a church stove
And the crabs walks in like people…

She laughs, and says, "Owww, *shit!*"*

---

*I'm not certain this is exactly what the last two lines were. Readers should feel free to work out a better transcription. All I know is that they made Bogan yell for us what may be one of the very first living *shit*s in recorded history.

But few audiences caught either Kennedy's grunt or this bootleg record, and the traditional sense of propriety reigned on. The aforementioned *Sad Sack* soldier in the comics was named from the expression "sad sack of shit," and in the early entries of the 1940s, it's almost disturbing how weary and melancholy everybody looks—you can almost smell the malaise wafting up from the page. But, still, not a hint of the word. In 1951, in *The Catcher in the Rye*, Holden Caulfield, so fertile with *damn*s and *hell*s and growling about "phonies," never once calls anything or anyone "shit," as a real-life prep school teen surely would have.

Other countries offer an instructive contrast. As far back as 1877, in his novel *L'Assommoir* about working-class Parisians, Émile Zola liberally used the French for *shit*, *piss*, *fuck*, and *butt* (*fesses*). It occasioned a degree of complaint among the prissier sorts but hardly kept the novel from publication and was by no means central to its success in creating scandal. Meanwhile, it would have been impossible for even "naturalistic" American writers like William Dean Howells and Theodore Dreiser to dip into such lexicon.

When the Code fell away and *shit* did start making it into the movies, it was sometimes awkwardly rendered, like a baby giraffe learning to walk. To me, the most resonant new usage comes in *Shaft* in 1971, with a weirdish running joke where people keep saying things like "Close it yourself, shitty!" The line feels fake. How often do we address *people* as "shitty" as opposed to saying that *things* are shitty? "Watch out, shitty"?

Nah—what someone in real life would have said then, as now, was "Close it yourself, you piece of shit."

Even though it was Woodstock-adjacent, 1971 was closer in time to the creaky talkies of 1929 than it is to when you are reading this. Aging producers still calling the shots had been minted in the black-and-white era, and old-school actors like William Holden, who had played the hunk in *Sunset Boulevard* in 1950, could still score leading roles in films like *Network* and *The Towering Inferno*. Only as the decade progressed did film start depicting *shit* and its variations with genuine frequency and gusto. You knew the word had been truly mainstreamed when in a jolly musical fable like 1982's *The Best Little Whorehouse in Texas*, Burt Reynolds's character warned Dom DeLuise's, "I'll beat you down so far you'll have to roll down your socks to take a shit!"

And yet, only recently have we escaped the prissy bind of having to choose between highfalutin euphemistic terms like *feces* or crude or juvenile ones. *Feces* has the air of a laboratory, *shit* of a lavatory, and specifically one at a zoo. *Kaka*, *doodoo*, *dukey*, and such are children's words. *BM* has approached status as a "normal" term—it's what I grew up with, for one—but it is a tad archaic of late, was never universal, and always leaned in the direction of "tootsies" for feet. Were sophisticated young adults circa 1962 sitting in sunken living rooms with their highballs referring to "BMs"?

But now we have *poop*. This one has lately jumped the rails from the kiddie terms to a neutral one, in the same way that *veggies* has. This is no accident: it signals that bodily matters are considered crucially less taboo than they once were, with slurs having become our true profanity.

The Grammar They Don't Tell You About

In any case, as a verb, *shit* has a quirk: What exactly is the past tense form, would you say? The Middle English form was *shote*, but that's clearly lost today. One is tempted to substitute *shitted*, but it doesn't feel quite right. What likely comes to mind is *shat*, but that also always feels arch, "not real," and in a way it isn't. The change from *shote* to *shat* was modeled on how we put *sit* in the past tense: *sit, sat*, and so *shit, shat*. However, this only happened about two hundred years ago and seems to have been intended with precisely the air of play that we feel in it today.

The truth is that *shit* is a defective verb. It has no unironic, vanilla past tense form that doesn't make you giggle a bit, which is why some readers are surely thinking that the real past tense form is "took a shit"!

Nevertheless, what this little word lacks in tense marking it more than makes up for in how multifarious it has been otherwise. It has come to mean so very much more than, well, a stool, and far beyond the extended meaning of "stuff" (*Get your shit out of my room*).

Let's start with an analogy. The multifarious array of flora and fauna in this world emerged via step-by-step evolutionary pathways that we can schematize as a family tree. In the same way, the full efflorescence of what *shit* can mean is so vast that it can seem a kind of chaos. Yet the bloom actually lends itself to, of all things, an elegant analysis, whereby a humble word accreted a magnificent but systematic cobble of meanings.

Linguists have a way of charting evolutions of this kind; it is a common process, hardly limited to peculiar, notorious, or salacious words. It's all about metaphorical extensions, and a prototypical example is the word *back*. You likely think first of your own back. Yes—that indeed is where it all began, the original, core meaning. But one of the foundations of the human language faculty is metaphor, and a word like *back* cannot just sit with that single meaning when it is so handy as a way of conveying others. *Back* flowered into what we could treat as three main directions.

First, it came to refer to not just the anatomical but to position—since your back is behind you, it was natural to refer to things as being in back, in the back of, even when no human body's back was involved. This positional usage led, through further metaphor, to referring to past time. If the past is behind us, then we might also say that something happened three years *back*, that we wish we could go *back* in time.

Back also became a way to reference support for someone or something. To have someone's back means that you are literally behind them to block them from falling down in some way. There is a short step to speaking of *backing* someone up, and then *backing* up an argument—and just think how far we have come, from the area below your shoulder blades to "You've got to back that up—I need facts!"

The third direction goes even further—just what is "back" about *back* in *The cat came back*? The idea is that someone has started out, and then turned backward, thus coming back. Hence to give something *back* is to reverse its original direction—i.e., back to you. This all means that *back in an hour* silently references what you can get talked about behind or stabbed in.

This diagram shows the true family relationship of *back* in a way that a list can only approximate:

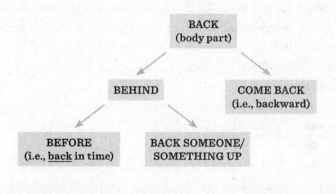

BACK
(body part)

BEHIND

COME BACK
(i.e., backward)

BEFORE
(i.e., back in time)

BACK SOMEONE/
SOMETHING UP

The Real Shit

Shit lends itself to equivalent treatment, and yields a diagram much richer, almost as if bearing out the nature of a word that can refer to fertilizer (sometimes so enthusiastically that you need a surplus supply shipped in, kept nice and dry above the waterline!). We get four metaphorical directions that explain pretty much all the ways we use the word in everyday language.

Extension 1—Feces Is Unwelcome

The metaphorical meaning closest to the root connotation of *feces* is that of the unwelcome, given the noxious nature of the substance. Hence the idea of haranguing someone as giving them shit. When I was in college, one of the managers in a dining hall I worked in was a brilliantined fellow with a pencil mustache (a look that was already obsolete by the 1980s) and a keening, petulant voice, given to complaining, "Everybody shits on me!"* But the man is relevant to us in that the expression he was so fond of embodied this metaphorical usage of shit as a burden, an insult.

Extension 2—Feces Is Real

But then, in a fashion few of us would think of immediately but makes a certain sense, we also associate shit with authenticity, with "the real." That babies, the most unfiltered form of humanity, have no control over it is part of where this sentiment comes

---

*One worker was known for a rather deft imitation of this man.†

†It was me.

from. Too, there is its universality despite its lowliness—it serves as a kind of demotic unifier, revealing the mundane in any individual regardless of exterior accoutrement or achievement.

Hence the expression that someone very good at something is "the shit," as in not some amateur but the real thing. That expression seems to have started with Black Americans—I first caught it in the 1980s from Black American persons—but not only has it jumped over the past few decades into general parlance, but this idea of shit as "real" was mainstream long before, in the expression "the real shit." Why is this how we designate the best music, the most potent hashish, or whatever someone has locked away for special occasions?

Note also the related usage, where someone who is knowledgeable about something "really knows their shit." Try translating these usages into any other language and get a sense of how odd they are despite how familiar we are with them. Yet they cohere as linked to a matter of essence.

So cozily has this extension of the meaning settled into English that it has become, of all things, a new pronoun of sorts. We get our shit together: note the parallel with "get our*selves* together"—we use *shit* to refer to that most authentic of the authentic, the self. In a sense we refer to our shit as the essence of ourselves, that which we, to set our lives on the right path, must get together, gather, make right.

That usage pops up in other ways—*Watch out with that; it'll fuck your shit up* does not refer to *shit* as in stuff. That drug will not merely disorganize your nightstand drawer but harm you at your personal core. As I write this, a few nights ago I saw two guys walking down the street, one of whom seemed somewhat into his cups. When he tripped stepping up onto a curb, the friend said, "Watch your shit!" This clearly referred neither to the man's possessions nor his bowels—it meant simply "Watch your*self*."

Although this usage may now seem exotic when viewed through the other end of the telescope, there are similar cases elsewhere. In and around Papua New Guinea is spoken a language called Tok Pisin, used as a lingua franca by people who speak hundreds of indigenous languages. Tok Pisin's origins were with the English settlement of Australia in the late eighteenth century, when a makeshift lingo using a few hundred English words, a few Australian ones, and the rudiments of the grammars of Australian languages emerged. That lingo was eventually used with people of what is now Papua New Guinea (the eastern half of the island called New Guinea) and islanders throughout the South Seas. Over the ages, what began as a limited pidgin, useful for basic matters but little beyond, flowered into a language, complete with "real" grammar and dictionaries and such, a native tongue of local children. Today it comes in assorted flavors throughout the region, and the Tok Pisin variety (*Pisin* comes from *business*, rather than from what it might look like) is now the language of government in Papua New Guinea.

When non-English-speaking people picked up English words and roped them into use in the original pidgin, they often had little reason to know, or even need to know, the specifics of their meanings. *Mary* was used for *woman*, *by and by* was used for *will*, *altogether* meant *all*, and so on. This unfiltered, from-the-ground-up perspective on English had especially neat results with, of all things, *ass*. For one, in Tok Pisin it carries no sense of the profane or improper. The originators of the language picked the word up from the randy British settlers who tended not to be exactly prissy about linguistic usage, and thought of it as meaning, simply, buttocks.

As such an innocent word, it was ripe for morphing into other neutral words. In Tok Pisin that metaphor involved foundation, that the buttocks are the base—hardly a stretch. As such, in Tok Pisin the seat of government is rendered, quite officially, as the government's ass place! Or, since the base is where it all started, the home base so to speak, the term for your home village is also "ass place"—*asples*.

Thus it is less English than human to associate the rear end with origin, truth, and self. But acknowledging that this is how things are in English means that if we are honest about how it is spoken (in America, at least), then we need to revise our sense of how pronouns work. They are far richer than the grammar books would have it.

For one, *shit* provides us with an alternate-world table of reflexive pronouns that convey both person and number—like vanilla ones—but also an attitude toward the person or thing in question, conveying lowdown, unfiltered honesty (your shit). *Get your shit together* implies a sense of the self without illusions or proprieties. Your goals, your sense of whether they will be achieved, your relationships, warts and all, your temper, your wardrobe choices, your pits, all of it—your *shit*, man. And yes, it does work even when the evaluator is as biased as your own self, as in *I finally got my shit together, man!*

So—book English:

myself	ourselves
yourself	yourselves
himself, herself, itself	themselves

Real English:

NEUTRAL:		WARMLY FORTHRIGHT:	
myself	ourselves	my shit	our shit
yourself	yourselves	your shit	your (pl.) shit
himself, herself, itself	themselves	his shit, her shit	their shit
itself		its shit	

This is, I must note, our first slice into what will be a whole new schema of how pronouns work in the "authentic" English we hear, know, and use. Profanity affords us a window into English as she is truly spoke: stay tuned.

Extension 3—Feces Is Lowly

Meanwhile, the most prolific branch of the basic meaning is the one that channels the sense of shit, in its ickiness, as referring to denigration and belittlement. The most immediate offshoots are our designating something as "like shit" (*He dances like shit*), referring to someone as a shit, and using *shit* as an adjective either in the form *shitty* or even as the bare word itself, as in living *a shit life* (this is more popular in the United Kingdom than in the United States, where we would usually say *a shitty life*).

However, the extensions via denigration go far beyond these intuitive usages. Think of a typical American English sentence like *I don't put up with that shit*. We certainly intend no literal reference to shit; rather, we aim to convey a dismissive attitude toward whatever is at issue. *I can't stand that shit. That shit looks like it's seventy years old! I've seen that shit since last year, and I know it when I see it.* What *that shit* means is just "that." It's a way of saying *that* with an air of vulgar dismissal.

In other words, *that shit* is a pronoun—a naive documenter of English, possibly even having already noted the independent word *shit* itself, would hear "that shit" as nothing but a pronoun people use when vaguely peeved. Or, really, just when speaking casually without even being especially peeved, depending on whom it is. The pronominal essence becomes clear, even if misleadingly in the technical sense, in a sentence like *Shit ain't right*. It's short for "That shit ain't right," yes. But, wow, when in rapid speech *shit* is pronounced without *that* in this way, we are tantalizingly close to a mere *it*—"It ain't right"—as if *shit* shortened to *it* amid the hustle. The Martian observer might mistakenly think that in an earlier English, there was no *it*, but only the longer form *shit*—that *he, she*, and *it* came from *he, she*, and *shit*!

Extension 3.1—Lowly Means Humble

But this branch sprouts more meanings in mushroomlike fashion. We get into extensions of extensions, even. If feces is about the lowly, then a natural association is humility, and here is where we come to *shit* meaning one's possessions. The idea that what one packs when moving is one's "shit" makes perfect sense when we know that word's meanings ooch bit by bit via visceral sentiment.

The "stuff" usage stems from the fact that the way we use language means commanding what a linguist calls softeners, which start with expressions like *sort of* and *kind of* and "type thing," and, yes, *like*: *I thought it was sort of the first time anyone had come out and told her that*, we say. The *sort of* is a hedge that allows us to not seem too prosecutorial in pointing that out, especially if we thought she needed to be told. But softening permeates real-life expression far beyond isolatable bits like *sort of*. It's time to leave a party, but really, you can't just say, "I am leaving." Rather, you say—and actually *must* say, on the pain of seeming chilly and abrupt—"I'm gonna head out." There are two softeners here—both the just-one-of-the-gang *gonna* instead of *going to*, and especially *head out*, which is how American Anglophones depart from a social gathering in a nondisruptive way. "I'm going to let you go," we say to bring a phone call to an end, when the other person gave no indication of wanting to stop talking. Propriety doesn't allow the straightforward "I'm going to hang up now"—it would convey displeasure, just as if you "ended" an interview rather than "wrapping it up."

I need somewhere to put my shit conveys the same nuance—
it may seem "vulgar," but to refer to your "things" sounds a little
metallic in a colloquial situation. You could say "stuff," too—
something shaggy, *humble*, that is—but *shit* is even more so. *Six
months and he still hasn't gotten his shit out of here*—someone
could say this, David Mamet *American Buffalo*-style, of a loved
one, or dude to dude. The "shit" has a leveling function—we all
have junk like our underwear, phone chargers, and deodorant.

The humility extension yields yet another grade A usage, in
the eternal and ubiquitous *and shit*, or really *'n' shit*. So easy to
dismiss as a random vulgarity, *and shit* actually harbors a certain subtlety, due to the logical lines via which the word has
evolved. A ways back, people were wearing T-shirts that read,
"I is a college student." Ha ha—they present themselves as edu-
cated but can't conjugate the verb *to be*, or don't know that Black
English is not considered formal language. Around then, a pal
of mine found especially funny another T-shirt: "I am a college
student. And shit." He loved it because "and shit" seemed incon-
gruous with higher education, but *technically* . . .

Technically, if someone said that, it would make a certain
sense. State straight out "I am a college student" and it conveys
a certain aggression, an arrogance, given the status associated
with the position. One might also express that one is happy to
be in college because of assorted implications, such as upward
mobility and spending time with other students and all they
have to offer, or even enjoying the fact that you are one of the
only members of your family who has had the opportunity.

But who has the time to say all that? A fleet, vivid expression can do the heavy lifting for you. A handy one would be "and stuff"—as in, we all inhabit this context and are aware of all that goes along with being a college student, i.e., that stuff. But here is where the softening comes in. One wishes not only to call on that shared knowledge but also to convey that one does not feel superior in being connected to it.

What better way to convey that humility, with *shit* already referring to one's physical rubbish not to mention one's very self (recall: *get my shit together*), than with substituting "and shit" for the older "and stuff" (much older—*and stuff* goes back to when English was still spelled funny). *I'm a college student and all of that, well, shit you know that I don't need to specify, and I don't mean to sound too high-and-mighty but, well, I'll get a better job than someone who isn't a college student and . . . aw shucks, y'know . . . shit.*

One must, as a mensch, strike a humble pose.

Extension 3.2—Lowly Means Fake

Then *shit* is also fake, as we reflect in phrases like *don't shit me*. But as ordinary as that expression is, it's based on another metaphor of a metaphor: that one way of being lesser is to be inauthentic. Thus also the noun version, where we talk of someone telling you "some shit"—*He gave me some shit about it being illegal to make a left turn at that intersection.* The wondrous thing about this branch is that it means that *shit* lends itself to metaphorization as both real (*he's the shit*) and unreal (*don't give me that shit*). Language can be that way, such that *literally* is used to mean both "by the letter" and the opposite concept of "figuratively," à la *I was literally boiling to death* when you, of course, were not.

Extension 3.3—Lowly Means Worthless

We use *shit* in a way that channels that something lowly is of little value, is a nullity. *It's shit* would be the most basic expression, followed by *I don't give a shit.** Or *I got shit*—imagine an adult, potty-mouthed Charlie Brown, who got a handful of rocks while trick-or-treating, saying that rather than the neutral "I got a rock"—and also the way we use *for shit* as in *he can't run for shit* or *these shoes don't fit for shit*.

But an alternate magic happens on this branch, where speakers quietly reinterpret a chunk of language and yank it into new functions that would make no sense if the original one hadn't reigned before. The denigration-is-worthlessness metaphor first creates the intuitive *dumb as shit, pale as shit, mean*

---

*Or the more graphic *I don't give two shits*. On that, linguists, proclaiming that there is no such thing as "wrong language," are often asked if there's anything people say that irritates them. I must admit that this one does rub me the wrong way—for my taste, too graphic for how often some people use it. I don't wish to have that image summoned under anything less than the most urgent of circumstances. I'm quite aware that legions would disagree, do not hear the expression as sensually repellent, and think I should just get over it. And they are right—or I have no way of telling them they aren't that I could confidently back up with pure logic, which teaches us that judgmental attitudes about language are always arbitrary.

as shit. Those mean "very dumb," "very pale," "very mean," so possibly we will start using *as shit* to mean *very* even with positive matters.

So, if you can say *poor as shit* to mean impoverished, then it can feel right to say *rich as shit* to mean loaded, *happy as shit* to mean elated. There is no literal application here, naturally. But if we use *as shit* as an intensifier of lousy things, hardly thinking of the literal meaning of *shit* at all, then after a while we can wrap our heads around expressions like judging someone as "hot as shit."

Extension 4—Feces Is Intense

This last extension stems from the same kind of reinterpretation as the one that yields that magnificently senseless *happy / rich / hot as shit.* Why is it that we can say, "If you see one of those bastards, run like shit"? Or "If it overheats, fan it like shit till I get back with some water"? What do the negative associations of feces have to do with an intense and effective action?

Here, the issue is substitution, of a kind that makes sense only in light of previous circumstances. We can also use *like hell* in this function—*run like hell; fan it like hell.* Hell is an extreme setting, singular and feared, so it's hardly bizarre that it becomes a way of expressing extremity, as noted in chapter one. But then, colorful expressions have a way of fading in power. Yesterday's *inde-goddamn-pendent* is today's *inde-fuckin'-pendent,* yesterday's *I don't give a damn* is today's *I don't give a shit* (but please, not two), or even more currently *I don't give a fuck.*

In the same way, yesterday's *run like hell* becomes today's *run like shit* out of a sense that a fresher cuss was needed to get the heat across. Any literal meaning is irrelevant. What mattered was slipping in a word of equal power. These days, *run like fuck* is just as good if not better, despite making not a bit more sense.

As such, our grimy little word lends itself to a diagram like the one for boring *back*, as in:

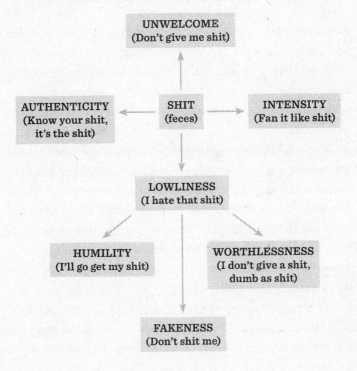

UNWELCOME
(Don't give me shit)

AUTHENTICITY
(Know your shit,
it's the shit)

SHIT
(feces)

INTENSITY
(Fan it like shit)

LOWLINESS
(I hate that shit)

HUMILITY
(I'll go get my shit)

WORTHLESSNESS
(I don't give a shit,
dumb as shit)

FAKENESS
(Don't shit me)

Who knew this was what *shit* is all about? One might adjudge the true nature of this word as *the shit* indeed. Curse words are not just vulgar and thoughtless. They morph and meander and slip according to predictable, and even elegant, contours of cognitive associations. A final metaphor, perhaps: *shit* is elegant!

The ABCs of Cursing

In science class we are taught that embryos go through stages that recapitulate the progression toward higher creatures. If what becomes a human had stepped off at an earlier subway stop, it would have been a fish, or at a later one, a crocodile, or at one farther on, a dog, and so on. Ontogeny recapitulates phylogeny.

In that profanity has traveled from being about God to about one's parts, one can see a kind of mirroring of that progression in how children process "bad words." I am watching it as I write this book. My seven-year-old is aware that I wrote what she knows as the "*fuck* chapter." Despite our fear that upon exposure to such words our children will shout them around, unaware of their taboo status, the truth is that kids easily sense that some words are hard liquor.

It's always been human to use words to not only refer directly to stuff (*house, run, red, in, maybe*) but also to apply social significance—used here and not there, at home but not at school, and that in the same way, some are dirty as opposed to normal. Our sense that kids acquire language as a succession of faceless words is a distortion, based on language fossilized in dictionaries, as opposed to its use in the roiling, socially multifarious real world.

Once, my older daughter popped off with "What the hell did that mean?" when my younger daughter created a nonsensical song. I was momentarily struck by her saying *hell* but decided not to correct it—*hell* is, quite simply, not profane anymore. I am probably a bit ahead of the permissiveness curve on that one, but I feel that we must allow that linguistic fashion changes.

However, my older daughter knows without anyone having told her that *fuck* is off-limits. She hears me using it here and there but knows she shouldn't, just as I knew in the 1970s that I was not to haul off with *hell*s the way my parents did. She is a good little postmedieval in this—the ones she treats as hot potatoes are the bodily bunch, even if she doesn't know what they refer to: *hell* is spicy but *fuck* is unthinkable. She also has a robust sense of what else is profane: the subject of the next chapter in Daddy's book, this one. I once asked her and a friend, "So what are some other bad words?" The two of them smugly said they knew them all—and listed "poop," "poopy" and "fart" before dissolving into laughter.

Lesson: they have internalized that matters anal—i.e., about the body—are profane. Their terminology will extend to *shit* soon enough. But they are largely past *damn* and *hell*, and blissfully naive of Profanity 3.0 of the *nigger* and *faggot* variety.

They are at an intermediate stage, titillated by what mature people a hundred years ago thought of as unspeakable in public.

To wit: the butt is piquant, as we also know from how sacred, in so many ways, is the status in our language of the word *ass*— to which we shall now proceed.

* 4 *

A KICK-*ASS*
LITTLE WORD

There's a funny thing that happens in English. You're at the zoo checking out some exotic-looking little horseish animals, wild asses of some sort, likely from somewhere in Asia. When your child asks what that horsey is you stifle a giggle as you tell them. It's an ass! An ass that you might ride, no less, whereupon you'd be doing so perched on your own, well, hee hee. What's with that, anyway—why are certain equines called the same thing as buttocks?

It is, as you might suppose, an accident. *Ass* referring to an animal goes way, way back, with similar words referring to animals that people made miserable. But *ass* referring to buttocks started as a fortuitously similar word, *arse*, which has a different origin story entirely. For Brits, *arse* still has a certain currency—recall the famous moment in *Pygmalion*, or *My Fair*

Lady, where Cockney Eliza gives her origins away at the races with "Move your bloody arse!"

The Ass-Place* of Ass

Arse shows itself confidently in ancient English. A nice early example is in early Middle English, in 1325, in a poem:

He nabbe nout a smok hire foule ers to hude.

which parsed out is:

She hadn't not a smock her foul arse to hide

as in, if we may, "She didn't have a smock to hide her dirty posterior."

The sentence, it must be noted, contains multitudes of factoids about earlier English, to the extent that the reader hankers for insights about how our language developed beyond the dirty stuff. If it's about a woman, why does it start with *he*? Because in Old English the words for *he* and *she* were alarmingly similar—*he* and *heo*—so after a while, in some places *heo* wore down to *he* leaving English a gender-neutral pronoun eons

---

*This subhead will make no sense if you happen to be sampling this chapter in isolation—see page 93.

before our current debates over *they*, *ze*, and beyond. Then what's *nabbe* for "didn't have"? In Old English, "I don't speak" was *Ic ne sprece*, and "I don't have" was *Ic ne hæbbe*, which became *Ic nabbe*, just as *Ic ne was*—"I was not"—became *Ic nas*! Middle English holds fun far beyond the *Canterbury Tales*.

In any case, note that the *ass* word contained an *r*. A key aspect of British English is that *r*'s have a way of dissolving—not when the *r* was at the beginning of a word (nobody in England calls rabbits "abbits"). But when the *r* is at the end of a word, or even close to the end, watch out—what began as *car* became "cah," *park* became "pahk."* Or at the end of a syllable—*Carson* pronounced as "Cah-son." It's key to what distinguishes British from American English. Note that *passel* and *bust* feel earthier than *parcel* and *burst*—that's because they started as *r*-less "mispronunciations" of exactly those words. *Hoss* for *horse* is a similar case from America, just as *ass* was a slangier *arse* over there.

The result was that likeness between the word for a horsey and the word for one's rump, and people were likely sensing it as early as Shakespeare. There are nuances of the time's linguistic scene that we will never be quite sure of. But goodness, he named his comic relief figure "Bottom" and then turned him

---

*Really, it's about syllables, not words. In *Parker*, the *r* didn't only fall off the end of the word and leave "Parr-kuh," but at the end of also the first syllable, too, so that it became the very old-school Received Pronunciation British "Pah-kuh." But to have noted that within the text would have been clumsy, especially after you indulged me without warning on the *heo* and *nabbe* business. You got the truth here.

into a donkey: "I am such a tender ass, if my hair do but tickle me, I must scratch." To suppose that the reference here was not anatomical would seem a bit prim.

Moreover, *donkey* only noses into English in the 1700s. Before that, donkeys were referred to as asses. There isn't a thing separating a donkey from one of those similarly medium-size zoo critters from Siberia, but at a certain point it felt improper to refer to the trotting of an ass, or the riding of one. One referred to someone making an ass of themselves, less because of anything so awful about donkeys than because of the accidental resemblance between their name and that of a butt.

In the early twentieth century, Booth Tarkington's literary reputation was roughly that of J. K. Rowling's and Jonathan Franzen's today, but nowadays he is largely and justifiably forgotten. Yet he is relevant to this book in a single thing he wrote: in 1898, he reported to his parents that his first impression upon becoming famous was that "I felt like a large gray Ass!—and looked like it." If *arse* for buttocks hadn't become identical to *ass* for horses, he'd have had no reason to liken his embarrassment to feeling like an equine. What, after all, is so definitionally embarrassing about being a modestly sized horse?

Underside and Underground

And it isn't an accident that *ass* clicked in as taboo in the 1700s, when the bourgeois sensibility that tabooed body parts was in full swing. Hence the delirious proliferation of euphemisms for the gluteus maximus. Before long, in Papua New Guinea they'd be saying *as* for *ass* (and *wul*—"hole"—for anus), but the English and Americans were distancing themselves via foreign-language words with the French *derrière*, or via studied vagueness with *backside* (yes, but which part of that back side?), *rear* (same thing), and *bottom* (of what? And how far down is it, really?).

Then there was the tailor's term *seat*, which used to get around more. George Jean Nathan, aristocratic theater reviewer of the mid-twentieth century and model for *All About Eve*'s Addison DeWitt, used it in a deliciously arch description of a low-grade World War II–era musical comedy aimed at soldiers, *Follow the Girls*, already mentioned in reference to *hell* in chapter two:

> *The fat comic reappears, curves his right hand over his head, and ejaculates, "What the hell!" Follow two hoofers who negotiate a fast dance, the woman partner singing a ditty called "You Don't Dance" and the male partner, at the conclusion of the hoofing, drolly kicking her in the seat.*

---

*The superciliousness is magnificent, especially given what overkill it was of the subject. The comic "ejaculates" what he says—the usage is legal but rare, and Nathan knew it. The hoofers "negotiate" their dance, implying a coarse trick rather than the tapper's intent to make at least something of a statement transcending the mere muscular. The song is a "ditty," and it's about *not* dancing even though they were dancing. The humble hoofing "concludes" rather than ends. And just what does it mean to kick someone in the butt "drolly"? (The comic was Jackie Gleason, for the record.)

So: "in the seat," "in the pants," but in 1943, not "in the ass."

The Jewish version was to cloak the word first with Yiddish and then with the "rear" deflection. *Tuchus*, a word used most in reference to children but also playfully for an adult, is Yiddish's rendition of the Hebrew word *toches* meaning "under," perhaps more familiar to Hebrew speakers today as the Israeli version *takhat*. It's neat how words just keep going—as a kid I attended schools where Jews were well represented and recall hearing the evolved version *tushy*. There's also the more common *tush*—both from a Hebrew word for "underneath"!

The closest pop culture gets before about 1965 is oblique references, and never regarding human adults. Typical were jokes about horses, especially when two people were in a horse costume and one of them complained about being the back end. In the silent film *Show People* from 1928, Marion Davies complains about always getting the butt part of the chicken, but even then, before the Production Code, she doesn't use that or any related word. Sometimes there'll be a visual joke about a baby's butt—think the business with the tattoo on same in the Danny Kaye comedy *The Court Jester*—but(t?) that's it. Not even the most vulgar, unforced characters, in even the grittiest black-and-white gangster pictures, could even say *ass*.

You could always depend on the Looney Tunes to push the envelope. When a character made a fool of himself, he would briefly turn into a donkey—i.e., an ass—and there was even some synergy with the gluteal meaning, in that the squawky, mocking five-note tune the orchestra played when this happened was known as "You're a Horse's Ass." But no character ever sang the words.

Today, of course, references to "booty" in popular music are ordinary, and *the* song, "Baby Got Back," is now so antique that a jolly but inattendant twentysomething dance teacher played it during one of my eight-year-old's gymnastics lessons. Back in the day, however, it was as if the gluteus maximus existed in childhood but was lost sometime before puberty. No pop songs about somebody having a big ol' butt, no Lucy asking Ricky whether a pair of dungarees made her buns look good, nobody in the beach blanket film series of the 1960s commenting on anybody's ass. People sang one another's praises about eyes, lips, and even legs, but it was as if people did not even have bottoms.*

Butt provided a transition point. By 1962, as the Production Code mores were fading, Paul Newman's skirt-chasing *Hud* character referred liberally to the body part. At one point he recalls pursuing "girlish butts," which sounded salty enough at the time but was a Hollywood euphemism for what that guy would really have said, along the lines of chasing "ass" or "asses." Straight-out references to *ass* were chasing up close *behind*, so to speak.

---

*An odd exception is in the forgotten musical of 1948 *Look Ma, I'm Dancin'*, which includes a lyric "Your little rear, I fear / Makes thousands leer." Very specific about that area for just after World War II. The rear in question belonged to, of all people, Nancy Walker, later famous as Rhoda Morgenstern's mother and Rosie of the Bounty paper towel commercials.

However, there is always a difference between the idealized and the genuine nature of this thing called language. Throughout the twentieth century, *ass*, while kept under wraps in polite society, was transforming the warp and woof of the language in quiet ways. String up Christmas lights in the afternoon and the result is some cords and dank little bulbs, a vulgar kind of intrusion you train yourself to look past. But at nightfall, switch them on and they not only outline but enhance the house, lend it some magic—you almost don't want to ever take them down. *Ass* is like that, if you know where to look.

Butt Anyway . . .

The essence of the word in English is that it harbors a certain potency. The nut is analogous to *shit*, the idea that excretion is unpleasant to a markedly high degree, and, in that, not only extreme, but also democratizing, in that none of us can claim exclusion from it.

I recall hearing a Pentecostal preacher sharing with a small congregation his insights on the humility we ought have before God, getting across that all of us create a certain redolence when evacuating, and that this redolence is us, Rolls-Royces or not, compared to the untainted, preternatural magnificence of the Lord. That depressing nugget conveyed that what goes on "down there" marks every individual among us as one of the flock. There can even be an affection in such a ranking, analogous to the fact that you might feel like you don't truly know, or love, someone until you've gotten drunk with them, sinking down to the same jolly level together.

It's that aspect (ass-pect? Last time, I swear) of things that has a way of seasoning a whole language, but the assorted meanings of *ass* have drifted so far beyond any gluteal connotation that it might be hard to fully feel the wonder of its pathway.

As such, it will be useful to start with that alternate term, *butt*. It has a vivid and almost tactile presence, partly because we process it as less profane. *Ass* makes us think "dirty," but *butt* is, while crude, more negotiable. Kiddies breaking up over butt jokes is cute, but we would blanch at them talking about asses. Dr. Seuss knew this. In the "Too Many Daves" after-story in *The Sneetches and Other Stories* book, he did a dazzling hypothetical of the names a mother should have given her twenty-three sons whom she, for some reason, gave all the same name, Dave. Imagine if she had called:

And one of them Sir Michael Carmichael Zutt
And one of them Oliver Boliver Butt

Generations of kids, I assume—on the basis of mine—have cherished the latter because it's about, well, butts. Yet if Seuss had submitted

And one of them Sir Michael Carmichael Cass
And one of them Dolliver Oliver Ass

113

Random House would have suggested a rephrasing, not only in 1961, but even now!

Consider then, the pathway via which a word like *butt*, so vividly referring to the posterior, can become a faceless piece of grammar. Back in the day, and even now, one referred to someone as *buck naked*, as in truly minus clothes. No one knows just what was intended via *buck*. Most likely the reference was to Black American or Native American young men, who in the 1800s and before were often referred to as "bucks" in a primitivizing way, and also associated with a certain unclad nature: Black men as slaves, Native Americans as attired the way some of them were in warmer weather.

In any case, the "buck" thing was hard to parse as time went by and ever fewer were familiar with African-descended persons working unwaged, or with Native Americans ever scarcer upon genocidal onslaught. After a while it seemed natural to suppose that the term was *"butt" naked*, as in naked to the point that one could see the butt. If *for all intents and purposes* can become *for all intentional purposes* (which I thought it was till after college) and *et cetera* can become *ekcetera* because so few people know Latin, then almost certainly *buck naked* will become *butt naked*.

But suppose at the same time as people are saying *butt naked* they are also saying *butt ugly*? Here, it isn't that *butt* started as some other word like *buck*. Rather, the intended meaning is that someone is as ugly as a posterior. "Butt ugly . . . ugly as a horse's butt!" I've heard people exclaim. English speakers will process two things here—1) *butt naked* means "really nude, not just with half your clothes off" and 2) *butt ugly* means very ugly, hideous. This means that as you go through life, with all that you have to think about, way back in your mind you start to process *butt*, of all things, as meaning *very*!

Won't you, then, without thinking about it, start using *butt* to mean *very* with other adjectives? I pose it as a question, but that's exactly what happened. *Butt cold* means "really cold," for example. It is no accident that *cold* is where that usage went— but only for a reason that links language change to the body. Did you ever notice that if you have occasion to place your hands upon someone else's naked posterior—oh, come on, most of us have at some point—that it tends to be a bit cooler than the rest of them? That's because the bottom maintains a lower temperature than the rest of the body, such that if you're cold, you may especially sense it in your bottom. This is why no one says "I'm butt hot."

I will never forget hearing in New York City circa 2002 a proper-speaking white woman of about twenty—her pale, sculpted, long-boned appearance would have fit in as a bit player in *Downton Abbey* or *The Crown*—saying to her date, "My ass is cold." She was attempting a certain Ebonics phrasing (her consort being African may have had something to do with that) and hardly meant that her buttocks alone were chilly. But then, she was indeed wearing a jacket that ended above the waist, it was indeed below freezing, and thus indeed her boo-tocks probably were especially cold.

Yet that took some evolution. Go back in time and say to the people in the Little House on the Prairie books "I'm butt cold." They would think you were referring to buttocks afflicted with what they called the ague, and would likely have you quietly exterminated as a mental defective.

Once *butt naked* and *butt ugly* were established for independent reasons, it feels right to think of *butt* as a way of heightening other things, especially ones related to the gluteal such as being chilly. What has happened to *ass* is the same kind of thing, but it's gone further.

Size Doesn't Always Matter (After a While)

One furrow *ass* has waddled down has led to a subtle but vivid nuance in our descriptive abilities. I refer to our use of it as a suffix with adjectives, as in *get yourself a big-ass pot* and *get a job with your broke-ass self.* This is one of those things that we are likely to misdescribe if asked about it. One might inform an English learner that *big-ass* means "really big," e.g., "It was a big-ass house!" But that's not quite right.

Not all of the *-ass* variations lend themselves to that description. "And they had this red-ass piano!" someone might remark—and note that they would not mean that the piano was an especially vibrant shade of tomato red. The word *remark* is key here: you would say red-ass piano as a way of conveying that you found the color not extreme, but remarkable, unexpected. Most pianos aren't red.

It's the same with *big-ass house*. You mean less that the house is gigantic than that it is large beyond what one would expect. *And he turned out to have this big-ass house* means that he turned out have, against expectation, a big house. Maybe you'd expected him to have a bungalow, or live in an apartment.

This adjectival usage of *ass* conveys an attitude, then. It is these kinds of usages that challenge our ability to say quite what a word "means"—recall the discussion of the meaning of *even* in chapter one. We are in the realm of what linguists refer to with the clumsy term *pragmatics*, as opposed to semantics. Semantics marks meaning in the way that we are used to thinking of it: *cocktail*, past tense, *and*. Pragmatics marks *why* we are saying something: attitude, what's new versus what's old, what's pushing the envelope—hence *like, even, 'n' shit*, and adjectival *ass*. That traditional conceptions of grammar sideline or omit pragmatics is a historical accident, and makes it much harder than it should be for us to wrap our minds around so much of what we say every day.

However, part of the reason pragmatics is barely known beyond linguists and philosophers is that it's often subtle—it's the deep sea of how a language works. A word first gets pulled into the shallows of semantics: intuitive, very language arts. When *like* started being used in the way we often process as hiccuppy, it was used to mean "similarly to," "approximately"—*We need to smarten it up a bit, like.* Only after a while was it coaxed down into the inky depths of the pragmatic, where the approximative meaning is only dimly processible and the real function is to lend a note suggesting the unexpected, something worthy of attention. *He actually, like, stood up* does not mean that he only made it up into a crouch, but that his having stood up was interesting—typical pragmatics in distinguishing the novel from the same old same old. The original meaning of *like* echoes distantly only, in that you can process the sentence as involving someone presenting the standing up as a *kind of* exhibit, performance: "Here's what it was *like*." But that kind of pragmatic meaning is a vastly abstract extension from the more basic semantic one.

This is how adjectival *ass* happened. It would have started with *big* (or possibly, frankly, *fat*) where the idea that someone who is big might, as one facet of that largeness, have a big butt makes sense. But then came that certain slide: from *big-ass* referring to the bigness to referring to the novelty of the bigness—related, but different, notions. That was the transition from the semantic to the pragmatic, deeper, more abstract. And it meant that *ass* could also now convey counterexpectation, and thus be appended to any adjective. Soon, you had *silly-ass*, *snobby-ass*, and *raggedy-ass*, where the meaning was not simply "very" but, more specifically, "in a way that you wouldn't normally think it would be."

We have a suffix, then, that doesn't make it into the grammar books, conveying that something is unexpected. A weird thing is that if English were allowed to morph the way it wanted to, with no print, literacy, and class sentiments encouraging us to hew how it looks on paper at a particular stage in its existence, then there would be a final step for adjectival *ass*. To connote something as unexpected is close to the very essence of why you say anything, which means that it would be easy for that suffix to come to signal that you bothered to say it at all—as in indicating some quality about it. To wit: it could come to blankly mark a word as describing something rather than naming what it is— i.e., as what we know as an adjective.

As such, in future English, *ass* could spread to all adjectives and be how we know a word is one of them, just as -*ly* works with adverbs. Bigass, littleass, richass, poorass, greenass, long-ass, with *ass*less expressions like *red, white, and blue* or *black and white* as random fossils of a stage when all adjectives didn't take the *ass* suffix yet.*

Stage One, 1830	*a big-ass man*	a man with a large posterior
Stage Two, 1930	*a big-ass man*	a man of unexpected size
Stage Three, 2300	*a bigass man*	a big man, period

---

*If you think I'm being silly, our South Seas lingua franca Tok Pisin does exactly this: the word *fellow*, as *pela*, became a marker of adjectives in just this way. *Big* is *bikpela*, *small* is *smolpela*, *black* is *blakpela*, and so on. Makes you kind of want to learn some, no?

The Pronouns They Don't Tell You About

Ass has also figured in a way that makes English pronouns more complicated than any grammar book would teach.

We must consider a sentence like "And so I'm gonna fire your ass." Rather, it means that I am going to fire *you*. Except I phrase it as firing "your ass." Not your actual ass, but "yer ass." Think of this sentence with the blackboard blinders that distract us from how much fun language is and you suppose that *I'm gonna fire your ass* involves the verb *fire* and an "object," *ass*. But is *ass* in that sentence really an object?

Clearly not, in that there is no reference to acting upon someone's buttocks separated from the rest of them. Note also that the accent issue confirms that we are dealing with something beyond a simple object. *The boy ate the ham*—you put an accent on *ham*. But here, it isn't "I'm gonna fire your ASS," but "I'm gonna fire yer ass." That is, you accent *your ass* exactly the way you would accent—or better, unaccent—*you*.

This means that *your ass* means *you*, and thus *your ass* is a pronoun. You only notice the butt facet if you have occasion to think about it. No one sane would ever respond, "Okay, but even if my ass is fired, the rest of me will still be coming back to work, and I hope you won't mind me working assless."

There is more evidence that this usage of *ass* isn't literal. You can use these pronoun-*ass* complexes as subjects, too. *Their asses sure know how to fuckin' jam. It happens every time his ass drives his car*. Again, any literal interpretation of *ass* makes no blessed sense. *They* dance well. *He* is driving his car.

Finally, there is the issue of the plurality of asses. If *ass* carried its literal meaning in sentences like this, then no one could say, "I certainly hope record companies begin to send viruses in their spoofed files, then I can sue their ass." But any English speaker knows that's a normal sentence—despite that technically we would assume that if there were multiple people involved, as in *their*, then we are dealing in multiple asses. Why can we say sue *their ass* as if they all shared one butt? Clearly we have left Kansas, and *their ass* is an alternate pronoun to the vanilla *them*. Sue them, or sue their ass. Even though it's anatomically impossible to share one unless they were conjoined twins.

In yet another way, *ass* has been dragged into the churn that creates the pragmatic. Here, the attitude in question is not the counterintuitive but the dismissive, or less nastily, the humble. *I* and *me* are neutral. In real English, *my ass* subs for both of these when you want to connote humility, the democratic. Or, stepping outside of yourself, *you* is neutral, while *your ass* happens when you want to demote someone, even if to suggest familiarity.

I was once in an opera camp (yes, there are such things) where, as is common in such settings, there was a certain shortage of men. There were enough to play the lead and secondary roles, but beyond that, one had to hustle a bit. In one of the productions that summer, for a smaller part they dragged in the boyfriend of one of the female leads, whose formal job in the organization was clerical despite that he had a bit of stage experience. He was a Blacktino gentleman, and I remember him backstage saying to the other men, "They're so short on dudes they got my ass up in it!" He could have said, "They got me in it!" but the "my ass" was more articulate, connoting a warm humility at the feet of the serious opera students surrounding him.*

There's nothing peculiar in English about developing a pronoun involving the butt. In countless languages, the reflexive—*myself, yourself*, etc.—uses the word *body*, so that you say "I wash my body" for "I wash myself." From there, it's a short distance to making it more specific and using "butt." For example, in Nigeria, the Yoruba language uses "body" in this function, but somewhat eastward is the language Igbo, where the expression is "my buttocks"—at least in one variety of the language. Chinua Achebe's *Things Fall Apart* has a neat scene where a white man is speaking to locals, interpreted into Igbo

---

*"My ass" was "up" in it, too, playing, of all things, a saucy Brooklynese cop who only spoke. I did it in my best Lionel Stander. For those who want to know, it was *Street Scene*. And as to why I didn't get to play the angry father, well, it was political, and I had other singing roles at the camp that summer that compensated (almost) for my not getting to play Frank. Anybody staging that show: I have maybe about another ten years left during which I'll do you a thoroughly decent "Let Things Be Like They Always Was" or "I Loved Her, Too."

by someone who speaks this dialect that has "my buttocks" for "myself," and an Igbo jokes, "Your buttocks understand our language." Now, actually, that particular dialect only uses *butt* for *myself, yourself, himself,* etc.—you wouldn't say, "My buttocks understand you"—but the jibe nicely parallels how the same *butt* thing can spread from the reflexive to all pronouns. In today's Black English, one could smoothly say, "Your ass gets the way we talk!"

Some suppose that today's *ass* pronouns were in fact sparked by slaves who spoke Igbo, but it's a thin case. It's only one dialect among many of Igbo that uses *butt* that way; slaves brought to America spoke a great many languages besides Igbo, and there is no indication that Igbo slaves had any dominant impact over others. *Ass* could easily have drifted into becoming a pronoun in English all by itself, due to the basic sense of the hindquarters as (1) nasty, (2) universal, and thus (3) making us all the same. *Watch your shit* and *fire your ass* spring from the same well—a human one.

Let's build on what we started in the previous chapter on *shit*.

The first thing you have to know is that what I call real English has two flavors of reflexive pronouns—neutral and affectionate: *myself* versus *my shit*, getting my shit together, where clearly the issue is not assembling your feces, but your *self*, which you love in all of its lowly essence.

But also, with the default, nonreflexive pronouns—just *I*,

you, *she*, *we*, etc.—English has another two kinds, whether they are subject or object. There's vanilla (*They even have me in it*) and dismissive (*They even have my ass in it*). If we laid it out as if it were in a grand old grammar book it would go:

NEUTRAL	DISMISSIVE	REFLEXIVE	INTIMATE REFLEXIVE
I / me	my ass	myself	my shit
you	your ass	yourself	your shit
he / him	his ass	himself	his shit
she / her	her ass	herself	her shit
we / us	our asses	ourselves	our shit
y'all	your asses	yourselves	your shit
they / them	their asses	themselves	their shit

But this is incomplete, in that the *it* is missing. We use *it* a lot—is it excluded from the fun here? No—but it involves, of all things, an irregularity, as jagged as things like *thought* instead of "thinked" and *was* instead of "be'd."

Namely, the way we express that dismissive tone is not as *its ass*: nobody says, "Pollen? I don't care about its ass." Rather, one says, "Pollen? I don't care about that shit." That's how we convey dismissal about an "it." And note that it's just like "your ass" in that we don't say "that SHIT," but "that shit" with no accent. It's a pronoun, in other words, despite the literal, and now lost, meaning.

So, *that shit doesn't even matter*; *I don't care about that shit*; (*that*) *shit's not right*—all of that is an entry into our grammar-book schema of how real, modern spoken English works, that a Martian analyst would set themselves to learn, unaware of our classification of certain words as "dirty." Observe:

NEUTRAL	"REAL"
No, I *saw* him.	No, I *saw* his ass.
No, I *saw* her.	No, I *saw* her ass.
No, I *saw* it.	No, I *saw* that shit.

It's irregular, in that it "should" be "its ass" rather than "that shit." But all languages have dings, and this is one of ours.

So, the full rundown of how pronouns work in the way legions of Anglophones speak English is:

NEUTRAL	DISMISSIVE	REFLEXIVE	INTIMATE REFLEXIVE
I / me	my ass	myself	my shit
you	your ass	yourself	your shit
he / him	his ass	himself	his shit
she / her	her ass	herself	her shit
it	**that shit**	itself	
we / us	our asses	ourselves	our shit
y'all	your asses	yourselves	your shit
they / them	their asses	themselves	their shit

There is a gap. No one says "its shit." That usage is about the personal, and an *it* is a thing, not a person. Recall that there is no real past tense form of *shit*, either—in so many ways, it's a quirky word. It's a smudge. The truth is that there are even dismissive pronouns in nothing less than the Old Testament, in the language it was written in first. Quick lesson: in Hebrew *that* is *zeh* for masculine nouns and *zot* for feminine ones. But in some spots in the original text, one finds alternate forms for those words that connote two shades: (1) dismissal and (2) "slangy." So, they precisely render the demotic, colloquial, or if we may, "Ebonics" feel of this "your ass" business.

In 1 Samuel 14:1 we read, "Come let us cross over to the Philistine garrison on that side." In Hebrew one says "side that" rather than "that side," so the text has:

me'ever   **hallaz**
from side   **that**
"from that crappy side over there"

Where *hallaz* means "that" where ordinarily it would be the vanilla *zeh* (specifically here as *ha-zeh*). The *hallaz* is a diss, "vulgar" language from the ordinary, as in "those shits over there," underscored when a bit later the people in question are billed "those uncircumcised ones." Or, there is a passage in Genesis 37:19 with Joseph's brothers, who hate him. They say, "Behold, that dreamer comes," and the original rendering of *that dreamer* is

ha-khalomot **hallazeh**
the dreamer **that**
"that there dreamer"

That *hallaz* business again—so opaque to us, but a streetish dismissal to anyone who knew Hebrew at the time. One could render that piece of Hebrew Bible scripture in today's American English as "Here comes Jo-jo wit' his dreamy ass!"

The Hole Thing

A discussion of *ass* is incomplete without stopping in on one of its most beloved derivatives: *asshole*. Yet again, that word starts semantic and goes pragmatic.

Asshole, in the sense we know, is later than we might intuit. Any film or television show set before the late 1960s in which a character calls someone an asshole is technically anachronistic. We can only know this by zeroing in on what an asshole truly is. There is evidence of similar usage to ours in English long, long ago—but *asshole* as we use it now runs deeper than mere anatomical comparison.

Is an asshole simply someone we don't like and thus comparable to a certain orifice? Not quite, and here's how we know. If you happen not to like musicals, you might be happy never to experience that there is a musical all about the men and women who have tried to assassinate presidents of the United States,

Assassins, with music by Stephen Sondheim. At a certain point, Squeaky Fromme keeps saying that the child of Sara Jane Moore, who, like Fromme, tried to kill Gerald Ford, is "an asshole." Why is it so pointedly funny to accuse a kid of being an asshole if *asshole* simply refers to an annoying person? If Fromme had said the kid was a pain it wouldn't be funny— *asshole* is loaded and thus a great line. Why?

As masterful public linguist Geoffrey Nunberg gets across in his *The Ascent of the A-Word*, followed more recently by Aaron James's *Assholes: A Theory*, an asshole is something very specific. He (and yes, he—we will get to the gender issue anon) transgresses while knowing that he is doing something wrong. The essence of an asshole is cutting in front of you in traffic. A little kid, then, can't be an asshole because he doesn't know moral parameters, any more than a cat can be an asshole, only perhaps seeming so via our tendency to overestimate their mental sophistication. We can't be assholes until we are roughly ten years old. The essence of an asshole is contravening the expected.

Expectation, what is normal versus what is novel—we are in pragmatics territory again, and as so often, this pragmatic meaning emerged from what began as a less abstract *semantic* one. Big surprise: *asshole* started as a metaphorical extension, to people tarred as just, well, shitty! That's the way it was as late as the 1950s when we first find *asshole* used in any way remotely resembling ours, in a description of God making people after which "there was a big pile of ass-holes left over. It looks to me like the Almighty just threw them ass-holes together, and made the Easton family." But the speaker means just "jerks," "doo-doo heads," in a story collected in a book called *Pissing in the Snow*. James Baldwin provides another proto-*asshole* in 1962 in his novel *Another Country*, in a character grumbling of a certain father: "Of course, he's an asshole too." But the person in question is weak, inattendant to certain grimy realities—a dud.

Only starting in the late seventies did this "dud" meaning deepen from the semantic—smelly—to the pragmatic—as in, a specific judgment about expectations versus reality, less blunt than a matter of "Pyew!" For a while the old and new meanings coexisted. *The Deer Hunter* of 1978, depicting events some years earlier, is invaluable here. It shows men in the early seventies talking realistically, where Christopher Walken's Nick and Robert De Niro's Mike use *asshole* to mean "weak one" (today, their likelier slur would be *pussy*). As vividly grimy as the film is, this usage is now dated—it's the less abstract old-school version, roughly "shitty"—rather than ours, which is about being a single facet of shittiness, a brazen transgressor:

NICK: *I sound like some asshole, right?*

MIKE: *I tell you Nick, you're the only guy I go hunting with, you know. I like a guy with quick moves and speed. I ain't gonna hunt with no assholes.*

NICK: *Well, who's an asshole?*

MIKE: *Who's an asshole? Who do you think is an asshole? They're all a bunch of assholes. I mean, I love 'em, they're great guys, but, you know, without you, I hunt alone. Seriously, that's what I'd do.*

They mean *asshole* as "fool." Only around this time was the word taking on a new connotation, more damning and condemnatory. The modern asshole is presumptuous, entitled—the key element is that he knows that he could do differently.

That is also a key element in the epithet *bitch* when applied to a woman—that the woman is culpable in the behavior in question, that on some level she knows "better." That usage is much older than *asshole*, which means that *asshole* came up behind *bitch* as a male equivalent of a concept once applied more readily to women. Certainly there were ways of referring to that kind of man before—in fact, the choice in America before *asshole* was *son of a bitch*.

Gil Perkins was a stuntman for star director John Ford's *The Informer* in 1935. Ford was notorious for recreationally challenging the men on his sets, and when he fired a blank wad from a gun into his face during a shootout take, Perkins objected, "For such a big shot, you're an inconsiderate son of a bitch!" As in, Ford knew what he did was wrong but figured he could get away with it. Note that phrasing it that way would sound antique if, say, Brad Pitt or Owen Wilson got mad at Quentin Tarantino. Those modern guys would call Tarantino, for the same kind of offense, an asshole, not a son of a bitch.

But this is why it feels a little creative to refer to a woman as an asshole, and why *bitch*, if applied to a man, has various meanings, none of which entail that he has committed offense while knowing better. It is as if English "wants" to have especially vibrant and explicit ways of calling people on the sin of self-aware transgression, complete with a gender distinction.

Everything's Bottoms

We will close this chapter by marveling yet again, after all we have seen, at how far and wide the word *ass* has evolved in English from its humble beginnings. Just as *pretzel*, *bra*, and *brachial* all trace back to a fertile word that originally meant "short," today a word that began in referring to the hindquarters is here a pronoun and there a suffix indicating mild surprise.

This is wild even from the perspective of other dialects of English, in which the trajectory has been similar but different. Our discussion has not occasioned an address of yet another pathway *ass* has gone down, referring to getting the best of someone physically: *They kicked his ass* almost never refers to something like silent film clowns kicking someone "in the seat." Rather, this usage is the spawn of the same thing that allows us to associate shit with authenticity. If *watch your shit* can mean "watch yourself," then it isn't that long a distance from there to *kick your ass* meaning to kick your real self, to beat you up.

The old Britcom *Fawlty Towers* gave a precious glimpse at

the fundamental weirdness of this idiom, in that it doesn't go through as readily in British, or, did not when this show was minted several decades ago. John Cleese's prissy, obsequious hotelier Basil Fawlty has a grouchy American customer* who isn't up for the drowsy, approximate service typical at the place, and especially doesn't like that the cook hasn't delivered the Waldorf salad he, wanting his mid-twentieth-century American comfort food, has demanded.

AMERICAN: *Tell 'im if he doesn't get on the ball, you're gonna bust his ass!*

BASIL: *Bust his…?*

AMERICAN: *I'll tell 'im!*

BASIL: *No, no, no! I'll tell him. Leave it to me! I've got it, I've got it, I've got it, I've got it, I've got it! Bust his…?*

AMERICAN: *Ass!*

BASIL: *Oh, that! Right.*

---

*This actor's American accent seems oddly off—turns out he was Canadian. I wonder what version of American he thought he was doing. British actors these days stun Americans with how well they do our accent(s), but they weren't as good at it before satellite television and home video steeped kids all over the world in Americanese early. I imagine that on that *Fawlty Towers* set in the seventies, the guy's version sounded good enough.

"Oh, that," Basil says, thinking of the actual body part—and he never stops, trying to wangle the expression with clunky, overly literal variants such as telling the cook (miming this for the American, as the cook isn't actually back there in the kitchen) "I'm going to break your bottom," or reporting, "I just smashed his backside about it," etc. After the American erupts once more with a "bust your ass," Basil tosses off a sidebar "Everything's bottoms, isn't it?"

Irresistibly we ask what it is about being American that led us to drive *ass* into such abstract connotations while everybody else just lets it speak for itself. German, for instance, makes lusty use of *Arsch* in cursing, but it always means either what it means, or the natural variation "idiot," with their *asshole* word, *Arschloch*, being the same. In German *Arschloch* is still used the way the guys in *The Deer Hunter* were using it in America almost fifty years ago. *Arsch* concerns neither counterexpectation nor vulnerability, nor has it acquired any real estate in the pronoun neighborhood. It just means "butt."

In the end, the American fetish falls within the bounds of normal humanity. Russian, for instance, makes rather a lot out of their word for *ass*. Overall, Russians curse a lot like Americans in many ways—they just assign the terminology differently. Our *deep shit* is the Russian's *deep ass*. "*Go to hell!*" in Miami; "*Go to ass!*" in Moscow. Lost off in some shithole near St. Paul? Near St. Petersburg you'd be lost off in some butt. Not quite as profoundly removed from the original meaning as in

English, but clearly within the spirit. And what the Russians do with their word for the male member can give English's *ass* a run for its money any day.

Not that English's own word for that body part hasn't seen a lot of life in its time, as we now shall look in on.

* 5 *

THOSE
CERTAIN PARTS

We have hands. More formally we might call them manual extremities; in slang we might call them paws (*keep your paws off her*) or mitts (*keep your grungy mitts off that pie*). But normally, neutrally: hands.

Some of us have penises; others of us have vaginas. But while *hand* is a word that traces endlessly back in time to Old English and beyond, *penis* and *vagina* are both Latin words that English primly took on only in the 1600s. Both are a tad formal. We teach them as more what one *calls* the parts than as what they *are called* spontaneously. There is, up high, *penis*, and then, down low, so many other terms that we likely learn first. The child knows *peepee*, and later assorted words he uses with a naughty snicker. *Penis* is not one of them: he dutifully internalizes that one as Sunday best, alien to chatting with his friends. Similarly, a girl quickly learns that what she has been instructed to *term* a vagina is more colloquially called other things with a giggle (*vajayjay*) or at least a certain willful insouciance (*vadge*) and beyond (*pussy*).

What English lacks is neutral terms for those two parts. There is *penis* and there is *dick*, but no vanilla term in between. The anatomist's *manual extremity*, the everyday *hand*, the grungy *mitt. Ocular organ* above *eye* above *peeper. Abdomen, stomach, belly.* But *penis* yields instantly to *dick*, *vagina* instantly to *pussy*. The Old English speaker had the vanilla: a man had a pintel. A woman had a sheath and later, frankly, a cunt, a term as ordinary at the time as oatmeal.

But after the Renaissance, notions of privacy rendered terms for genitals profane. Hence one either euphemized with foreign words or cawed on the barstool with vulgar ones, in a language that now lacked simple, honest words for the genital organs.

It's the same with the *anus*, if I may. I recall a speaker of a language of the Himalayas who was a graduate student in America and a thoroughly fluent but non-native-English speaker. In a linguistics class he offered a useful insight on how words' meanings change over time, when he made reference to *assholes*. He was referring to words for anus, and genuinely did not know that the English word he had heard most in that meaning was not one a native speaker would consider appropriate for reference, especially repeatedly, in the formal setting of a classroom.

But he was an innocent. If he had said *anuses*, we would process it as too formal and hear him as the quaint foreigner. He said *asshole*, and we giggled—yet what was he supposed to say? What would have been "right"? *Butthole?* There is no term that would have worked. Whereas, in his language, there is a neutral word for anus, less formal than that one, but less vulgar than *asshole*. His language is normal—English, in rendering *asshole* taboo, is weird.

We modern Anglophones can barely imagine the purpose of neutral terms for "down there." Arms and hands are one thing, but penises and vaginas? Certainly, for the respectable person the choice is between antimacassar dissimulation and sassy gutter talk. But that's our modern nature talking. For our most ordinary words for genitals to be not mundane but profane is a modern business, based on how the profanity spotlight shifted from the religious to the corporeal. The result: snickery words like *dick* and *pussy*. Roll the dice again, and in a society in which the profanity spotlight moved in different directions, those words would be as neutral as *arm* and *hand*. Instead, they are nasty.

Dick: What Was It About Richard?

The array of slang terms for the penis is almost bedazzling, and I would no more venture to address them all than to address all the known terms for being drunk. *Prick*, *John Thomas*, *tallywhacker, weiner, tool, organ, pecker, wang*, and so on and on (and on). It's usually fairly clear what motivated the reference, and less clear just when the usage began, given that notions of propriety discouraged the writing of such terms until the twentieth century.

Of course, some of the terms' origins are less clear than others'. I suspect *wang* was on the wane by the time I hit college—I haven't heard it since 1983. However, it was short for *whang-doodle*, one of various equivalents of "whatchamacallit," used heavily enough as a euphemism for that certain thing that it was shortened affectionately over time.

Then there is the priggish *member*. You'd assume that the original meaning was today's main one, referring to someone in a club, but actually it referred to a part of the body. This meaning specialized in two directions. One was metaphorical, applying the sense of an arm's membership on a body to a person's membership in the Raccoon Lodge. The other was to restrict *member* to a particular body part—yes, that one.

And *weiner, tool*? We'll leave those aside—too easy. More interesting is the king of the penile terms, *dick*—interesting partly in that it is, in contrast to the above terms, a "dirty" word.

It all starts with the name Richard. Richard became Rick, which then became Dick because of something medieval English speakers found jocular that only proves that humor dates badly. To them, changing the first consonant to create a nickname was cute. Robert to Bob, William to Bill, Margaret to Meg to Peg—ha *ha*! But what we want to know is why the organ was named on the basis of this particular nickname, Dick, as opposed to, say, Walter.

That a name would furnish the slang term is easier to understand: we have always leaned toward a certain anthropomorphization of the penis. The independent liveliness of the thing has something to do with that, as well as aspects of its shape, what with the "head" and all. The same likeness spurred other terms such as *Peter*, *Willie*, *Johnson*, and *John Thomas*, but *Dick* won out.

Dick first, however, did a stopover between nickname and sexual term, as a generic term that meant roughly "fella." It conveyed a harmlessly unremarkable sort of person, a meaning preserved today in the expression *Tom, Dick, and Harry*. Its usage paralleled, roughly, that of *guy* today, as in a remark in 1592 about "a brave dapper Dick, quaintly attired in velvet and satin," or Shakespeare referring in *Two Gentlemen of Verona* to a sly, charming "dick that smiles" and "knows the trick to make my lady laugh."

The official verdict is that *dick* only started referring to the penis in the late nineteenth century, but this is based on a rather unyielding reading of the evidence. As early as the 1600s, the word is used often in obvious double entendres poised sweetly between the "guy" meaning and the one we know. "Who," a book titled appropriately *Wit and Mirth* asked in 1691, "had not rather kiss the Breeches of Twenty Women, than to lick the Bristles of one Male dear Dick?" We are hardly snickering schoolboys to sense that the bristles in question are meant to put us in mind of a certain area of a man's person. "For when Country Gillians do play with their Dicks, Then London must Father their Bastards." Nominally, the "Gillians" are playing with "guys," but our immediate sense of a saltier meaning would likely not have been alien to people of 1707 when the jape was written. In fact, if "guy" was the only meaning, the statement is oddly flat. The double meaning gives it basic life, a spark of creation.

For my money, the first clear usage of *dick* as anatomy is in 1654, with this savory putdown: "You can ... lie like a logge by me all Night, and when you rise, turn your back-side towards me, as though I should kiss that: out thou unnaturall Knave thou; thou feeble dick thou." Can we really believe that the meaning here is just "you feeble *fellow*"? The capitalization gives it away. We are in the era when people were more improvisatory about it than today, but note that *night* and *knave* get the capital but *dick* does not. We would expect it, of all the words in this sentence, to be capitalized if the reference were merely to the name "Dick" in the sense of "Tom, Dick, and Harry." When this woman said "feeble dick," she meant, well, what she meant!

But it is true that in 1888 we get the first absolutely crystal clear reference to what could only possibly be the body part, with no indirection or ambiguity. It pops up in a collection of salty vignettes, tossed in so casually that we know the word had been in common parlance for eons before. One thinks "What took you so long?" when marveling that a baby just born, so clearly human and ready for prime time, was until now secluded from us, bobbling in fluid. Welcome, *dick*—we were beginning to wonder.

The scene in the book is an anecdote, in which sometime during the Benjamin Harrison administration a lass is on a lad's lap facing forward, with a certain frottage going on. He turns her around to face him, described in the stage action, so to speak, as "turning her fairly around and putting his dick where his finger was."

"Nice, isn't it, ducky?" he chirps, in a text that makes it clear that the terms *prick* and *cunt* were also already in full swing as we know them today.

Penetrating the Language

As bad words have a way of doing, after *dick* hit the ground as an anatomical reference, the metaphors started roiling up and folding into the language. Just as if *shit* is worthless, then it will come to substitute for *nothing* (*I got shit*), then if we don't exactly rank penises in value alongside our dining room crystal, then *dick* will mean "nothing" as well. Hence *He doesn't know dick*. The first recorded example is in the 1920s, but I'd put money on that workers ages before on the First Transcontinental Railroad were saying "You ain't gettin' dick, brother!" We'll never know for sure, but get a look at John Ford's 1924 silent *The Iron Horse*, an almost granular depiction of the building of that railroad,* and note how hard it is to confidently suppose that people in that setting, if you went back in time and cawed, "They didn't give me dick for all that gold I found!" would turn and marvel, "Tarnation, I love that sonuvabitch's gutbucket queer turns o' phrase!"

Dick once just meant "some guy," but through the penile meaning came to refer to a more specific type of man—a jerk. The *Oxford English Dictionary*'s first usage of this kind is in the novel *Seventh Avenue* by Norman Bogner, a big enough hit in America in 1967 that it was made into a television miniseries. "He's a dick," a character grumbles when a camp counselor makes him and his mates line up for inspection.**

But if the anatomical reference had been around for so long, wouldn't it have been tempting from the get-go to call "dicks" those whom the *OED* perfectly terms "knowingly obnoxious"? Why didn't this usage hit the page until Lyndon Johnson was

---

*I know—"Get a look" as if I were writing about some juicy forties noir any film fan would want to catch rather than some forgotten silent film. But I almost mean it—this is one of the few silents beyond the Chaplin/Keaton/*Phantom of the Opera*/*Metropolis* warhorses that, if you have developed a decent pair of "olde-filtering" glasses, almost holds up. Start roughly in the middle, since it's a long one, and note that you actually care when the railroad crews, working each from opposite sides of the United States, finally meet and a single railroad now binds the nation.

**The counselor is "Uncle Don," which makes me recall, amid the endless indignities of 1970s day camp with the warm cartons of milk, shirtless athletic activities, and pissing-contest atmosphere, how one was to call camp counselors "Uncle" who clearly would rather have been doing other things with their summer.

being undone by Vietnam? Because another term had already crept into the slot: *prick*.

As early as 1598, when *dick* was still poised somewhere between "fella" and "organ," a proto-lexicographer was listing *prick* as synonymous with words meaning roughly "jackass" such as *pillicock, primcock, gull, noddie* (i.e., a dupe), and *prettie lad*, at a time when *pretty* could convey a diss, a meaning now only recoverable from "Things have come to a pretty pass when . . ." Later, in 1822, the indefatigable William Hazlitt griped in a letter, "Her putting up with this prick of a fellow, merely for bore and measurement and gross manners, sets me low indeed."

Languages, for the record, differ in which nasty words they rope into meaning, basically, everything. We have seen how English fetishizes *fuck, shit,* and *ass* beyond what culture alone could explain. Others give *dick* pride of place.

For a very long time I had the unusual experience of getting my hair cut by a Haitian in a shop owned by a Russian speaker. I would enjoy trying to understand as much as I could of the Haitian's talk with friends dropping by while also trying to get as much of the sneery, muscle-shirted Russian guy's endless palaver with his own pals. The latter never worked too well, and a good half of the problem was that I couldn't parse the profanity. That was because *dick* (as well as *ass* and *pussy,* but that's another story) is so engrained in the real language that you just have to "be there" to comprehend, and once every two months for forty-five minutes isn't "there" enough.

However, from consulting the page and seeing this business tamed into sedentary print, I savor that in Russian, well, observe:

ENGLISH	RUSSIAN
zero, zip	not a dick
nothing in particular	no special dick
beat him up	dick him up
light into someone	up and dick someone
smash to pieces	dick to pieces
Are you crazy?	Are you torn off your dick?
shittily	dickly
random, shoddy crap	dickery
Not on your life!	A dick up your ass!
Who knows?	Dick knows.
No way!	Dick to you!
out the wazoo	up to dick
It's the same either way	Same dick.
I'll be goddamned!	Not even a dick do I have!
twiddle your thumbs	swing your dick at a pear tree
To hell with him.	———————

There are indeed wrong answers but I assume you can fill in that last one, as in to where—or actually, what—Russians send the person in question! Or, one of my favorites is that to shoot the shit, as in to talk about "this and that," is to talk about what we could render as "penis/me-ness." The Russian expression uses their *dick* word, but there's no way to use ours in an English translation that gets the "me" aspect in. Russians: I refer to *xujo-mojo*.

Rooster Is a Neologism?

Dick shares space not only with obviously less au courant terms such as *Johnson*, but also with a term I would likely center this chapter on if I were writing fifty years ago or before: *cock*. However, that word is, in the grand scheme of things, a loser. It has not burrowed into the language the way *dick* has. A guy who cuts you off in traffic may be a dick, but he isn't a cock. Nor do we say that someone doesn't know cock about gambling. In British English *cock* has been used alongside *dick* in the meaning of roughly "fella" and still is—*the old cock* used to be a common expression, and you can still hear, "How's it going, cock?"—but that is about as far as it goes.

In terms of access to the spicier lanes of meaning, *cock* has been cockblocked by *dick*. Yet time was that *cock* was the default slang term for penis, elbowing *dick* into the shadows the way dinosaurs kept early mammals rat-size and nocturnal. In 1578, when we have to make do with oblique references to *dick*, a play has a guy priding himself on his deftness says that "cock for my gain doth stand," as in his deftness can be symbolized by an erection. "Oh man, what art thou, when thy cock is up?" asks a widow in a play in 1618.

But why *cock* to begin with? You will recall that *fuck*'s lineage may trace at least in part to the Vikings; with *cock*, that pedigree is clearer. The original word was *pillecock*, a borrowing from words like the now forgotten Danish *pillerkok*. In Danish and Norwegian, the *pill* part meant "penis"; the rest was garnish that meant "little." However, just as *hamburger* began as referring to meat prepared in a way originating supposedly in Hamburg but was misinterpreted as combining *ham* and a new word, *burger*, English speakers interpreted the *cock* in *pillecock* as containing the core meaning, with the *pille* part as some unidentifiable prelude.

Likely, the barnyard fowl "cock" encouraged this interpretation. In Old English, that meaning had extended metaphorically to a self-satisfied kind of lad strutting about, and as we have seen, there is a straight line from references to people to references to the member. Plus there are still English speakers who refer to the penis as a "bird." (I heard this from a Black American of Baltimore in 1987; surely she was not an outlier.)

So why not just assume *cock* meaning "penis" started with chickens without bringing in this strange Scandinavian word now unknown? Because despite how arcane and beside the point it seems to us now, *pillecock* appears first and often; *cock* in the sexual meaning is later. For a spell—the same one during which men were gliding around named Fuckbutter and being taken seriously—there were even people named the likes of Jo-hanne Pilecoc. (Were these blithely smutty last names in the 1100s and 1200s due to some kind of cultural fatigue after the Norman takeover?)

In any case, once *cock* was established as sexual, its other meanings started peeling away like friends snubbing someone charged with embezzlement. *Rooster*, for example, only emerged in the 1700s, and as a euphemism à la "chest" for *breasts*. A male chicken was once a "roost cock," but once *cock* was icky, *rooster* was subbed in. A cock was also a little pipe on a barrel that liquid came out of. Note that *spigot* and *faucet* are, despite their ordinariness, Frenchy. We use them when people stopped call-ing what water (or beer) came out of a cock; Brits chose *tap* for the same reason. In a different world, *Little Women* was written by Louisa May Alcox—but her father had changed his name. No cocks for him.

You never know what will happen to a word from place to place. In some varieties of English, *cock* hangs on with the old-school connotation. The Jamaican happily gives her child cock soup from a packet, named according to the Old English meaning of the word, with nary a thought of the packet containing penises. Think also of Scotland's cock-a-leekie soup. Then the good old "male chicken" meaning serves in the funniest sentence I have ever known, by a solid but non-native-English speaker who informs us that "Like English, Chinese is a language without gender, i.e., apart from the natural sex of the nouns such as *man, woman, boy, waitress, cock, bitch*, etc."

In these cases *cock* means chickens in general, rather than just male ones. But it may surprise you to know that in the United States, *cock* has sometimes been used to refer to the female as well as male pudendum. It's been a Southern, and therefore often Black American, thing. In 1902, a man described wind blowing a petticoat up such that "I saw my Lula's cock," while the Black tradition of insult trading called the Dozens included casual references to "your Mammy's cock." We need blues singer Lucille Bogan yet again, in 1935:

> *My back is made of whalebone*
> *And my cock is made of brass.*
> *And my fuckin' is made for workin' men's two dollars*
> *Bringin' God around to kiss my ass.*

This lasted into the late twentieth century—relatives of mine who grew up as late as the 1970s knowing *cock* as both penis and vagina were thrown to find that whites they met as they went out into the world only used it in reference to the male member.

For the record, old *pillecock* less died than morphed. It long ago streamlined into *pillock*, known in the United Kingdom as a word for roughly doo-doo head. But meanwhile, with *cock*, in America the basic penile meaning has reigned on through the centuries, such that as late as 1965, Kurt Vonnegut, in *God Bless*

You, Mr. Rosewater, wrote a father yelling "Drop your cocks and grab your socks" to his sons to summon them to boat-deck labor.

More likely today the character would say something like "Drop your dicks and hit the bricks," just as by 2003 in the gloriously smutty musical *Avenue Q*'s "The Internet Is for Porn" Trekkie Monster so memorably grunted, "Grab your dick and double-click" to sample online pornography. These days, forget anyone bored flinging their "cocks" at a pear tree or anything else.

I have lived just long enough to witness the transition. I probably first encountered *cock* as used by a female college friend, who was given to talking about them a fair amount. But this was in the early eighties, which were the final years of Vonnegut's usage. By as soon afterward as the late eighties, I'm pretty sure her equivalent was saying *dick*; by the nineties, the word would have marked someone as past thirty or beyond. I learned to smoke *pot* in the eighties; teens before me in the seventies smoked *grass*; today I date myself in not calling it *weed*. *Cock* yielded to *dick* according to the same vagary of fashion. One today hears of "dick deets" (as in details about a new lover's you-know), but not "cock docs," or whatever the expression would have been if *cock* had stayed current.

Cock did not disappear, however. *Cash* first referred to a money box and only later to what was in it. But *cash* now has an even narrower space in the language, either referring to paper money as specifically contrasted with checks and credit cards, or used with an implication of vulgar abundance ("Plus, he's got the cash"). *Cock* has undergone that kind of narrowing, as the linguist calls it—starting as "male member," but winding up as, these days, more specifically "male member in a pornographic context." This is why we don't hear "Drop your cocks and grab your socks" today. If it isn't a silver-haired gent sipping a martini saying it, then one assumes it's from a paragraph in a *Penthouse Forum* "letter." These days, "drop your cocks" has an implication of desiring said cocks, whereas Vonnegut meant no such thing. Neither in locker rooms, barracks, nor "guy talk" are *cocks* at issue as opposed to *dicks*: today, *cock* is to porn as *bouquet* is to wine.

Pussy: Here, Kitty, Kitty

Out of the animal kingdom, the penis tends to attract names of birds (with allowance made for occasional terms like *dog*). For the vagina, the references tend to be cuddlier. In a comparative mood, it would appear that cats, especially, have a way of getting people going.

I refer, of course, to *pussy*. A certain parallel in texture and warmth is clear. Add a feeling of fondness and pinch of privacy—note how one tends to place one's face close to cats and talk to them with pursed lips as if the exchange is somehow exclusive—and the question is almost why there would *not* have arisen a feline term.

The first anatomical reference on paper is in 1699, and, wouldn't you know, in the same *Wit and Mirth* that lends us the first attestation of *dick*. The setting is a poem in which a man of a certain age marries a teenaged lady who is agitated that he doesn't "feed" her "pussey." The gentleman dutifully fetches a younger man more up to the job and:

> He took it to stroak it
> And close in his Lap
> He laid it to feed it
> And gave it some Pap.

Okay, we get it! Of course this is double entendre winky, as the "feeble dick" passage probably was. The first direct example in print is the still shocking line in a pornographic tome of 1865, from which we garner that as far back as the year Abraham Lincoln was assassinated, a person could pen a passage such as "My poor pussy, rent and sore / Dreaded yet longed for one fuck more."

There is a theory that the sexual reference did not come into existence until around the time of that passage and that the smattering of earlier references must be one-off creativities. This interpretation is based on the fact that long before that, *pussy* was used as an ordinary term of endearment for women. For example, in 1583 a Puritan pamphleteer in England grouses that "you shall have every saucy boy, of ten, fourteen, sixteen, or twenty years of age, catch up with a woman, and marry her, without any fear of God at all . . . so he have his pretty pussy to huggle withall, for that is the only thing he desireth."

Pussy in this sense can indeed throw us off. When our modern normal is the underpants gnome on an earlyish episode of *South Park* battling Cartman and chirping, "That all you got, pussy?" it's downright weird to read Little Eva's father in *Uncle Tom's Cabin* asking her, "What do you think, pussy?" meaning "baby girl" or "sweetie." However, the idea that this rules out that people were also using it as a sexual reference founders on the eternal misimpression that humans cannot handle related but distinct meanings in a word. The visual image we cannot escape, of words and sentences in cold print, distracts us from how profoundly bound in context language is in living, casual exchange.

We need only consult today's situation with the N-word, where legions of people Black and beyond casually use it as a term of endearment quite aware of its alternate usage as a slur, bemused by observers' claim to hear the two usages as the same word. To get more directly analogous, we must recall men going about in serene confidence named Dick, as in both of the actors who played Darrin on *Bewitched*, Dicks York and Sargent. Neither are on record as having been socially hobbled by their first names sounding like what was in their pants.

Surely, then, one could call one's sweetheart "pussy" while the same word was used for, well, one *part* of your sweetheart in other contexts. Likely the homophony lent itself to flirty wordplay, unrecorded for posterity. Consider Madonna to Dick Tracy on the soundtrack album of the film—by 1990 she could purr, "Dick—that's an interesting name." More to the point, Edna St. Vincent Millay's husband was given to references to his wife's "kitty," while surely thinking of no such thing when calling a cat.

The evidence suggests, then, that not just Abraham Lincoln but likely George Washington and possibly even Oliver Cromwell were familiar with *pussy* as a sexual term. I wouldn't be surprised if it goes back even further, to the initial invaders of England from the Continent, and thus back to before English was even English. Low German is, confusingly, actually spoken in the top half of Germany, and is essentially a different language from High German. It has *puse* for both the feline and the anatomical reference. The nature of things means that its speakers may have noticed the likeness independently of English speakers—after all, French uses its cat word *chat* in a similar way. But the traditional analysis of such commonalities from the same root is to assume that they inherited a double meaning from the single language that birthed them both. In the case of the progenitor language of English and Low German, it was spoken a minimum of two thousand years back.

That may be pushing it, but almost certainly the anatomical reference in English was not a neologism as the boys were coming back from the Civil and/or Crimean Wars. Otherwise, we have to imagine that the 1699 story about the "stroking" was just a labored joke for readers who had never encountered the cat comparison before. And even if we can manage that, then what do we do with a 1790 poetic line that goes:

Thro' Susan's Holland smock or spare
Or on her pussie for to stare.

A Holland smock is a garment; Susan is a woman; and crucially, a spare was a slit in a garment. Are we to believe that the person eyeing Susan in this prurient manner considers beholding her house cat an equivalent pleasure one might randomly opt for instead? Just because people lived a while ago and spelled funny doesn't mean they were incoherent, and it's safe to assume that the "pussie" here was what we would "thinke."

I would be remiss not to mention that some propose that the anatomical reference came from the Vikings, whose Old Norse included a word *puss* that meant "pouch." However, this derivation, which so seems what some lonely Victorian bachelor philologist would come up with by candlelight, is as tenuous as it is depressing, whereas the cat one is neither of these things. Pouches or pussycats? Come now.

Pussy Galore

The genital meaning is but one of *pussy*'s evolutions over the centuries: it has also come to be used as a name one calls someone. That name has taken its place alongside *dick* as a judgmental one on males: the *dick* is a jerk, while the *pussy* is a coward. American Sign Language neatly illustrates this evolution, with the coward meaning of *pussy* indicated by making the sign for vagina accompanied by a frown (or, depending on the context, derisive smile).

In fact, though, the evolution in English was a little less direct. The coward meaning comes to us courtesy of the sadly common series of associations whereby homosexuality is linked to weakness. Step one, the source, was the affectionate usage with women we have already seen. This came to be used as a disrespectful term for gay men by, at least, the twentieth century. Lawrence Durrell lent a late example of this now obsolete usage in one of his Alexandria Quartet books, in which writer Percy Pursewarden notes that he once met Henry James at a brothel with a "naked houri on each knee" and that he therefore surmises that James was a "pussy." Then, in the same way that in modern American slang *that's so gay* has been used to tar something as unsuitable, after the 1950s, *pussy* morphed from referring to gay men to referring to any man perceived as lacking in courage. Certainly the anatomical reference, and the disrespect associated with it, played a cross-fertilizing role here.

The result is a lesson in the eternal question of where our words come from. A word for *cat* is now first, one for a body part, and then, one used in judgment of men rather than women, having detoured through first being used to refer to women themselves and then to homosexual men.

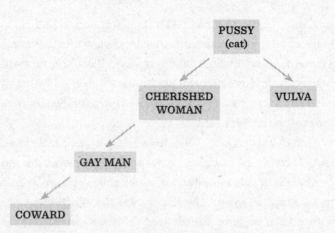

Heedless, and often heartless, aggregate creativity across the eons is what drives the birth of words. After all, this all started with cats!

Over Here versus Over There

There is always an unpredictable aspect to how language changes. For example, Dick persisted as a common name until quite recently with no one batting an eye, while *cock* quickly had everyone clutching their pearls and ditching the word's original meanings. This kind of chance variation can also distinguish dialects of a language, and a case in point is the fate of *pussy* on the two sides of the Atlantic.

In the United States, one knows intellectually that *pussy* refers to cats. However, I wonder whether that sense is kept alive mostly by childhood immersion in, specifically, Sylvester and Tweety cartoons and Tweety's talk of "putty tats." I submit that few Americans these days refer to cats as pussies, and that *pussycat* is a word both well-known and faintly archaic. As I write, my children, five and eight, despite their ample lexicons, only know cats are "pussies" from my immersing them in Looney Tunes. In 2020, my sense of the word *pussy* is that even if one tries to use it in a feline reference, it occasions at least a bit of a snicker—often from oneself. The sexual reference has essentially taken over. (Meanwhile, in England one can refer casually to a "bitch puppy" despite knowing what *bitch* can mean otherwise, while Americans would have to work not to spit out their wine. We know that *bitch* "means" "female dog," but that "meaning" is now an archival matter, learned mainly when someone around ten asks what *son of a bitch* means.)

Hence when Donald Trump, during his first campaign for president, was revealed to have recounted of women that he had been given leave to "grab 'em by the pussy," it was widely thought that his campaign was finished. This was in part because of how inconceivable it seemed to many that someone could be elected president after having not only referred to the action, but using the relevant word. A president we can play back at the push of a button saying *pussy*? The incongruity we sensed here revealed the word as profane, not just naughty. Or: today it would be quite beyond me to read out loud Edward Lear's lovely "Owl and the Pussy-Cat" poem where anyone who knew the sexual meaning could hear it. That is, it might be okay for a child, but otherwise, I cannot hear this poem with the casual sense of separation from the sexual meaning that people manage when thinking of Dick Van Dyke:

> The Owl and the Pussy-cat went to sea
>> In a beautiful pea-green boat,
> They took some honey, and plenty of money,
>> Wrapped up in a five-pound note.
> The Owl looked up to the stars above,
>> And sang to a small guitar,
> "O lovely Pussy! O Pussy, my love,
> What a beautiful Pussy you are,
>> You are,
>> You are!
> What a beautiful Pussy you are!"

Yet matters are again different in Britain, where the sexual meaning surely hangs over but seems not to utterly eliminate the animal one. I will never forget when I first fell in love with the Britcom *Are You Being Served?* in the early nineties, and heard Mrs. Slocombe sound off with "Having a bath at six o'clock in the morning played havoc with my pussy!" (the episode was "No Sale"). As always in the scripts, she quickly said something that let you in that she was referring to her cat, but I thought, "Wait, did she just say *pussy* with even a double entendre *implication*?"

Mrs. Slocombe regularly made references to her "pussy" in this way ("Mr. Humphries, leave my pussy alone!"), and even though the joke highlighted the double meaning, what is crucial is that no American show in the same era could even have ventured there. Imagine Betty White as Sue Ann Nivens on *The Mary Tyler Moore Show* circa 1975, as sexualized as the character was, grinningly saying something to her crush Lou Grant about a "pussy" while discussing her calico at home. It would have been unthinkable then, even after Woodstock, streakers, and even in one early episode after an oblique reference to Mary taking the pill. To say *pussy* here feels plain dirty, rather than like straddling a line.

In the 1920s, there was a British pop song called, of all things, "My Girl's Pussy." (It was released in 1931, but the song is pure twenties.) As it happened, the lyric dwelled on the same joke as the sexual term's print debut in that poem about the "pussey"—"I stroke it every chance I get," "no matter what the weather's like, it's always nice and warm," and even the intriguing "seldom plays and never purrs."* Pure Mrs. Slocombe decades earlier and again, meant as a joke, but no American song

---

*Thanks to Ken Teutsch for turning me on to this song.

could have gotten away with it at all—it would have sounded like it meant only one thing, not two.

The difference is simply that the animal term retreated in America more quickly than in Britain, for reasons likely as unchartable as why nobody drinks lemonade in Finland.* To understand how language changes without allowing a certain space for serendipity is to understand it not at all.

The C-Word: From Anatomy to Animadversion

Some readers may have wondered why I did not discuss this word right after the exploration of *dick*. The reason is that in common usage, its anatomical reference has become somewhat abstract, in the same way that the animal reference of *pussy* is in American English. That *cunt* is a word for the female genitalia is a fact that we know, but in actual usage, the word resonates more as a vicious slur.

As scornfully as it can be used, *pussy* harbors always a certain air of play, as a diminutive word ending in -*y*, and originally

---

*They don't—or at least they didn't in Helsinki in 2005. I looked everywhere over six weeks, and was always greeted with looks as if I had asked for onion daiquiri mix. They had other fruit juices, but lemon juice with sugar just hadn't made its way into the culture for what can only be due, given how luscious lemonade is, to chance. You can't get, for the same nonreason, chicken broth in stores in Denmark.

referring to a charming animal. *Cunt* is starker, meaner—it just sits, neither diminutive nor recalling an endearing creature, and stings even harder in being applied to the sex that has already undergone so much. Devalued since the dawn of the species as mere sexual objects and breeders of children, the woman now receives an epithet that implies that her essence, once again, is her reproductive parts.

It is, in its way, perhaps a sign of progress, then, that this word is today the most taboo of the taboo words other than *nigger*. The days of *fuck* being treated as English's worst word are over, since specifically the feminist revolution of the 1970s. Before this, taboo though the word was, underground it was afforded more leeway. The annals of old show business, as always, are a handy window into that earlier reality. In her work with Lucille Ball, Vivian Vance—Ethel Mertz to her Lucy Ricardo—could be a tad touchy on set, never ecstatic that as an experienced stage actress she ended up eternally best known as a frumpy television sidekick. When guesting on *I Love Lucy* in 1957, actress and professionally irrepressible "personality" Tallulah Bankhead, experiencing Vance's aura, kept greeting her as "Cunty" on the set. In 1953, Cole Porter played a song he had written for his musical *Can-Can* for character actor Hans Conried. When Porter finished, Conried asked, "Is this song about a cunt?" Porter said yes, and Conried refused to perform it.

Stories like these give a peek at how real people communicated at the time, despite how language was represented on paper.* The significance of both of these stories is not their being funny (though they are) but that neither would be likely now. Even Roseanne Barr would not glide around a sitcom set calling anybody "Cunty," nor would Nathan Lane toss off references to cunts during rehearsals. *Cunt* is a slur, and slurs are today's true obscenity.

Out of the Mists

Almost as if the word was laying low due to its infamy, *cunt* has one of the murkiest etymologies of all the words of this book. At the end of the day, we simply don't know where this charmless little grunt of a word came from and possibly never will. It turns up in living color in early Middle English, as if it had always been around, which it likely had—but not leaving evidence for us.

---

*I have this story only from the liner notes of a recording of Porter songs by the highly arch producer Ben Bagley, and sometimes one wonders whether he was making some of his anecdotes like these up. However, this one just feels right to me in terms of what both Conried and Porter seem to have been like, and so I take the risk of repeating it here for posterity. The song, for the record, was "Her Heart Was in Her Work"—dig up the cut, performed in a cute working-class Brit accent by Lynn Redgrave. It's quite catchy. Or, more readily available online as I write is Porter himself doing it at the piano, a performance that nicely gets across exactly what Conried would have objected to.

As is typical of such words, we first meet it as unprofane. In 1505, a Scottish poem tells us:

The count of ane sow kis	The cunt of a sow to kiss
Is nocht bettir I wis	Is not better, I know
for the collik	For colic

One of the oddest things to encounter in English of that era is the word used casually as an anatomical term even in medical sources. "In women the neck of the bladder is short, and is made fast to the cunt," one text mentions around 1400. A homely proverb almost a century before that advises, in an English so early that it is barely the language we speak and thus requires translation, "Give your cunt wisely and make demands after the wedding."

By the way, Chaucer did not bedeck his *Canterbury Tales* with casual reference to cunts, despite how this gets around among English majors. It is easy to suppose, because Middle English spelling looks so odd to us and was not yet regularized, that his *queynte* was an eccentric spelling of *cunt*. However, it was actually what it looked like: the word *quaint*, which at the time referred to a dainty or precious thing, not having yet drifted into its current application to things vaguely tacky and possibly a tad low-class. Where Chaucer refers to women as having a "queynte," it is a pun—one frankly on the clumsy side—and not a direct reference.

This is especially clear in the Miller's Tale when he uses the word both straight and in humor:

As clerkes ben ful subtle and ful queynte,	As clerks are very ingenious and clever,
And prively he caughte hire by the queynte,	And discreetly he caught her by the "quaint,"
And seyde, "Ywis, but if ich have my wille,	And said, "Indeed, unless I have my will,
For deerne love of thee, lemman, I spille.	I will spill [dead] for secret love of you, dearie.

If the second *queynte* were really the word for vagina, then the first one means that Chaucer was saying that clerks are vaginas, which makes not a whit of sense. He was, rather, saying that clerks are foxy little numbers, in a time when the word for foxy little number happened to sound rather like the word for vagina, upon which he then in the next line referred to the vagina using the "foxy little number" word.

To sense how this would have played in Chaucer's time, we might imagine someone working a pun on boobs as "boots," as frankly I dimly recall someone in my orbit doing eons ago. Someone had some swanky boots on, but the surrounding conversation had lent attention to, well, something further up of a sort that she had a bent toward rendering rather salient, upon which the dialogue went something like, "Yes, I'm glad you like my *boots*. Oh, were we talking about my *boots*?"

Yes, it was forced. But really, the Chaucer pun wasn't much defter than this—again, humor dates badly. But it means that when the Wife of Bath says, "For certain, old dotard, by your leave / You shall have queynte enough at eve," she is making a joke—especially since a few lines later she coyly refers to the same thing in French as her "belle chose" (pretty thing). A better pun was from the Bard, who had Hamlet asking Ophelia, "Do you think I meant COUNTry matters?" and suggesting lying on her lap. But that's around 1600, long after we know the word existed.

We can trace it further back, the same way that we get a head-on look at post–Battle of Hastings *fuck* and *pillecock*: baldly potty-mouthed place names and even personal names. The Oxfordshire gentleman in 1230 might choose certain gratifications on what was openly titled Gropecuntlane, and this was but one of many streets in England of the period with names like this! Meanwhile, there were actual people who led actual lives with names like Gunka Cuntless, Belle Widecunt, John Fillcunt, and Simon Sitbythecunt.

Before even this? We can know that English got the word as DNA from its immediate family. Cognates sprinkle English's Germanic relatives—Icelandic has its *kunta*, Low German got into the act again in its Middle stage with *kunte*. The Dutch have *kont*, but for some reason the reference slipped backward to the hole nearby and now just connotes "butt," and gender neutrally to boot (to butt?). But a search before the Germanic brood to Europe's *paterfamilias* language is fruitless—the signal goes cold.

Latin, 'tis true, has a word *cunnus*, which not only means "wedge" but is related to a verb that meant "to squeeze in." Antennas go up—might *cunnus* and *cunt* (plus *kunta* and *kont* and the rest) suggest an ancestral word 6,500 years back or more? Not quite. Like various delectable linguistic propositions along the lines of shit boats, *fuck* starting as "fornication under consent of the king," and Dutch being the first language (yes, someone was actually ready to die on that hill), the *cunnus* origin story just doesn't go through.

There's a general—and mysterious—process that happened to Germanic languages at their single origin somewhere around Denmark called Grimm's law (it was discovered in part by Jacob Grimm, who otherwise collected for us the fairy tales more familiar from sanitized Disney versions). Basically, words that came from the big daddy language from Ukraine starting with crisp *p*, *t*, and *k* for some reason around Denmark became hissier: the tart click became something sounding like a fizz from a radiator, while in most of the other descendants of that tongue the sounds stayed perky. So—the *p* sound became an *f*, and hence Latin's *pater* and our *father*. The *t* sound became a *th*, and hence Latin's *tres* but our *three*. And the *k* sound became *h*, and hence their *canis* for dog became our *hound*, their *centum* for hundred became our, yes, *hundred*. So that means that if English got *cunt* from *cunnus*, it would be something like "hunt"—and it just isn't.

As such, we are left sifting around the Germanic languages, hoping to find some *cunt*ish word for the vagina (or thereabouts) that lots of them now have, or that maybe there was some earlier meaning that morphed into the vaginal one. That effort fails.

There is an athletic surmise that the source was *kuon*, which meant "cow." But while it's quite plausible that sniggering males would refer to women as cows (since they still do), I don't see them narrowing that down to referring to that specific anatomical part.

We will likely never know. All we have is a faint radio signal, amid which there seems to be something about roughly the syllable "coo." That alone has meant "vagina" here and there in English. More familiar today is *cooch*. Then comes *hoochie-coochie*, via our subconscious English pattern of prefixing already randomish and even nonsensical words with an echo version starting with *h* to have a little fun—*higgledy-piggledy, hocus-pocus, helter-skelter, hoochie-coochie*. Naturally come abbreviated versions of even this: *hooch*, the more affectionate or mocking *hoochie*, and finally terms such as *hoochie mama*, used by the late-twentieth century as a disparaging term for women associated with "the hood" with an antediluvian implication of what used to be termed *loose virtue*. This was then sometimes adapted to the likes of "ghetto hoochie" (as at least I recall from about 1997 in California).

Making It Personal

That was nasty, and spawn of the same sentiments that led our c-word to become the epithet that it is now. By the 1600s, *cunt* was being used as a passingly disrespectful word for women, rather equivalent to the streety "ho" of today. Diarist Samuel Pepys is of great use to us, describing a drunken Sir Charles Sedley in 1663 coming out naked onto a balcony and preaching a mock sermon, "acting all the postures of lust and buggery that could be imagined, and . . . saying that he hath to sell such a pouder as should make all the cunts in town run after him—a thousand people standing underneath to see and hear him." For the record, what happened after that: "And that being done, he took a glass of wine and washed his prick in it and then drank it off."*

From here on, the word was used regularly as a dismissive reference to women, sometimes with an air of "easy virtue" baked in, always brutally objectifying. In 1911, a man in a tavern of sorts was recorded by undercover officers as complaining that it had been hard to dance because "there was such a bunch of cunts dancing on the floor." The celebrated realism of novelist Henry Roth meant glumly genuine passages in the 1930s such

---

*I'm hard-pressed to decide whether I'd rather spend life in Restoration London or 1970s summer camp.

as "I sees a pretty cunt come walkin' up de street... wit' a mean shaft an' a sweet pair o' knockers." And after that, *le déluge*, narrowing into not just dismissal but fury.

Like *pussy*, the word has a different feel in America than in the United Kingdom and Australia. Its status in America as the quintessence of vulgarity and offense can throw these other Anglophones at first. I am pretty sure I have never even used it other than to refer to it in an academic sense. However, Brits casually throw it around as a mildly censorious epithet. It has joined *pussy* in jumping the fence to refer to men, but often with a shade of affection. Few things are more confusing to an American abroad than hearing (1) someone use *fuck off* to refer to someone just departing insouciantly and (2) a man calling a friend of his a "funny cunt."

The word has become a leveler along the lines of *son of a bitch* among American men a hundred years ago, *bastard* among them fifty years later, and today, especially when no Black people are listening, "nigga" picked up from hip-hop, as meanwhile Black men use *nigga* and *motherfucker* in the same usage. More specifically, listening to British men using *cunt* today, one gleans a term occupying a slot one part "nigga" and one part "bitches," the latter in the affectionately denigrating usage American men often use with one another.

Hence a truly weird pathway. *Cunt* starts as anatomical, becomes an epithet for persons bearing the anatomical part, and then becomes a term of affection for those who do not bear it. Add that in Dutch it just means "ass" and we get this diagram:

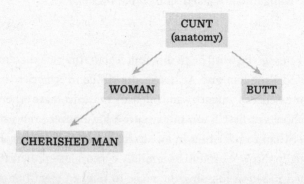

Rhymes with *Bunny*

If there is a way of leavening our discussion of as unpleasant a word as this one, it may serve as a palate cleanser to learn that *cunt* also had the peculiar legacy of determining why we call a certain long-eared, alertly blank creature a rabbit.

Did you ever notice that there is no word like it for that animal in any other language (unless you've been brushing up on your Middle West Flemish)? French for "rabbit" is not something like *le rabitte* but *lapin*. Germans have *Hase*, not *Das Rabbitchen*. Romans called it a *lepus*, not a *rabbitus*. What's with "rabbit"?

What we "should" call rabbits is *coneys*, which is what English speakers did call them at first. *Rabbit* began as the word for the juvenile version, which had about as much purchase on daily existence as the modern word for baby rabbits does now (*leveret* stew, anyone?). Coney—as in Spanish's *conejo*, Greek's *kouneli*, and so on—was the original. Another peek at Samuel Pepys's diary shows us why we had to let *coney* go.

Pepys had an appetite for venery, and his diary is full of recollections such as this one from 1668 about an assignation with his maid when "my wife, coming up suddenly, did find me imbracing the girl… and endeed, I was with my main [French for hand] in her cunny." "Cunny," then, a more faithful rendition of a word written as *coney*. Think of how *honey* and *money* are pronounced, and you not only get a new perspective on how *honey* is spelled in *Winnie-the-Pooh*, but also realize that Anglophones dined not on "KOH-neez" but "KUH-neez." Cats, we see, aren't the only animal that called to mind the vagina—the rabbit makes just as much sense.*

With the term now classified as vulgar, it wouldn't do to refer to cunnies hopping around the garden or furnishing a rib-sticking stew. By the 1800s, the baby term *rabbit*, once obscure-ish, had been dragged in to replace the now off-limits *coney*. Thus English has a peculiar and rather homely word for a markedly cute (if blank) animal because of the incursion of one for a genital.

---

*Except for the blankness, but oh well—I find rabbits stunningly clueless. Guinea pigs are really the same thing, but their nullity seems intuitive because they have small ears. They are naught but their oval little poo-popping whateverness. Somehow, the length and motility of rabbits' ears makes you expect a certain spunk, which they nevertheless resolutely lack.

* 6 *

WHY DO WE CALL IT
"THE N-WORD"?

Gone are the days when Allen Walker Read decreed in 1934 that *fuck* was "the word that has the deepest stigma of any in the language." In line with the strength of the taboo, he never wrote the word itself in the article. Today, however, a walk down a street, or a peek at every second film made, renders his assessment antique.

Not that no words carry such a prohibition in English today. These days, there are two that most writers would treat as Read did. One is *cunt*, and the other, possibly the most taboo word in this book is *nigger*.

Even writing it here, I sense myself as pushing the envelope—and feel a need to state that in this chapter I will be writing the word freely, rather than "the N-word." Am I taking advantage of the fact that I am Black, such that etiquette allows me a certain leverage? Yes indeed. I apologize for any discomfort it engenders but suspect that few readers or listeners would truly prefer that I follow Read's example and compose an entire chapter without naming what I am discussing, or write *the N-word* a hundred times. I will use it as sparingly as I can, but that will nevertheless leave a great many times when I do spell it out, love it though I shall not.

The Word That Shall Not Be Spoken

The word is indeed twenty-first-century English's Voldemort term, motivating, for example, an entire book by Black literature professor Jabari Asim titled *The N Word: Who Can Say It, Who Shouldn't, and Why*. When Black Harvard law professor Randall Kennedy wrote a book exploring its past and present power titled *Nigger* in 2002, many Black scholars and writers condemned him for possibly encouraging the word's acceptance.

Its public use can stain and even derail a career. In 2006, *Seinfeld*'s Kramer, Michael Richards, spewed it during a stand-up routine in an improvised rant against a Black heckler. It was an example of what linguists call reported speech, quoting a hypothetical person using the word, but even this once-removed utterance was received the way a medieval taking the Lord's name in vain would have been, with colleagues like Jerry Seinfeld discussing it with the gravity we would expect if Richards had been revealed as a pedophile.

In 2013, celebrity chef Paula Deen self-reported having used the word in anger after being held up by a Black man, and allowed that she had used it occasionally at other times as well, treating it as a bad habit that Southerners like her were getting past. The Food Network declined to renew her contract, and her career has only fitfully recovered.

It has become just as dangerous to even utter the word in reference or academic discussion. In 1968, James Baldwin proudly declared on *The Dick Cavett Show*, "I am not your nigger." But an acclaimed documentary on Baldwin in 2019 was carefully titled *I Am Not Your Negro*, and when literature professor Laurie Sheck ventured a discussion in a class at the New School on why Baldwin's phrasing had been elided, she uttered the word itself—only to be reported to the administration by students in her class. She narrowly avoided being fired as Paula Deen was.

It has even become risky to utter a word that *sounds* like it. In 1999, a white mayoral aide in Washington, DC, said in a meeting that it would be necessary to be niggardly with certain funds. Some of the staff members listening were Black and offended to the point that he was fired (although later reinstated). The resemblance between *niggardly* and *nigger* is accidental—*nig* meant "miser" in the Viking language brought to England—and of all the grievous associations with Blackness that we could enumerate, being miserly is not one of them. Just the sequence of sounds, regardless of meaning, offends deeply. Less widely aired was when just a month later, a Black undergraduate registered a complaint at the University of Wisconsin–Madison when an English professor used *niggardly* in a class—and this student had not been aware of the incident in Washington.

That is the power of the word in our times. It is much more than forbidden as an epithet. It has become a word that, even in the most abstract of senses, one is forbidden to utter at all. Although we tend not to label it as such, *nigger* is taboo, i.e., profanity. It is much more profane, in the actual sense, than *fuck*, *shit*, and *ass*, which we classify as "bad words" but make our peace with hearing daily (and probably use ourselves).

If my toddler daughter calls bird droppings "shit," or the younger one, already the professional wit of the two, refers to a rough blanket as "shitty" with a naughty glint in her eye, I wince with a smile. Neither use such words regularly; little ones drink in a sense of lexical appropriateness faster and better than we might suppose. However, if either of them referred to anyone as a "nigger," I would need therapy.

The word we are expected to refer to only with a euphemism: this is what the anthropologist recognizes as not just a "slur," but as *profanity*.

From Aethiops to Apple Pie

For all of its potency, in terms of etymology, *nigger* is on the dull side, like *damn* and *hell*. It just goes back to Latin's word for black, *niger*, which not surprisingly could refer to Africans, although Latin preferred alternatives like *aethiops*—a singular, not plural, word—which was borrowed from Greek where it meant (surprise again) "burn face."

English got the word more directly from Spanish's rendition of that *niger* word, *negro*, which they applied to Africans amid their "explorations." *Nigger* seems more like Latin's *niger* than Spanish's *negro*, but that's an accident—few English sailors and tradesmen were spending much time reading Cicero. *Nigger* is how an Englishman unconcerned with taking a stab at foreign words would say *negro*. For Mandarin's *fēngshui* we say "fung shway" as the Chinese do, but if the term had caught on in the 1500s or even the early 1900s, we would be pronouncing it more like "funk shoe-y," just as we say "chop suey" for something that is pronounced in Cantonese "tsopp suh-ew." In the same way, *Negro* to *nigger* is as *fellow* is to *feller*, or *Old Yellow* is to *Old Yeller*—*nigger* feels more natural in an Anglophone mouth than *Negro*.

Nigger first appears in English writings in the 1500s. As it happens, the first reference involves "Aethiops," which had come to refer to Ethiopia, or at least applied sloppily to Africa. We read of "The Nigers of Aethiop" in 1577, and that spelling is but one of many from then on: *neger, nigur, niger, nigor, nigre*—take your pick.

As late as the 1700s, the word is still somewhat of a novelty, when the average reader may not have actually met or even much discussed said "nigors." Scottish poet Robert Burns duti-fully taught, referring to a "niger," that it rhymes with "vigour, rigour, tiger." Note, we might, that last word, and how it explains a certain something relating to our slur of reference. If *tiger* rhymes with *vigor* and *rigor*, that means that *tiger* could once be pronounced "tigger," which then sheds light on that classic children's rhyme:

> *Eeny, meeny, miny, moe*
> *Catch a tiger by the toe*
> *If he hollers let him go*
> *Eeeny, meeny, miny, moe.*

Why would any sane person grab a tiger by the toe, when even grabbing a house cat in such a manner can guarantee having your palm slashed open? Do we really imagine a tiger "hollering" in protest as opposed to roaring?

"Tigger" was a polite substitute for an original *nigger*. So: for one, we gain insight into the *Winnie-the-Pooh* character and why the books are so vague on how his name is pronounced. More to the point, the original version of the "Eeny, meeny" doggerel is a window into how brutally casual the usage of *nigger* once was, happily trilled even by children at play. For centuries, it was the equivalent of today's "African American."

Someone writes in passing in 1656 that wooly hair is "very short as Nigers have," with the term meant as bland clinical reference. "Jethro, his Niger, was then taken," someone else writes in a diary twenty years later. This sort of thing goes on through the 1700s and 1800s. Just as *cunt* was a neutral ana-tomical term in medieval textbooks, *nigger*, however spelled, was simply the way one said "Black person." After a while, the current spelling settles in, which makes the contrast with today especially stark.

The period straddling the nineteenth and twentieth centu-ries is especially interesting, in that while America is becoming recognizable as its modern self, its denizens are using *nigger* as casually as today we use *soccer mom*. In Frank Norris's *Vando-ver and the Brute*, set at the end of the 1800s, the burgherly white protagonist in San Francisco is squiring a gal about town who has been doing some schoolteaching, and:

> told him about the funny little nigger girl, and about the games and songs and how they played birds and hopped around and cried, "Twit, twit," and the game of the butter-flies visiting the flowers.

She isn't hurling the label as a slur—it's just how one referred to a Black child in casual speech. Annals of popular dancing shortly after this era gaily chronicle dances such as the bunny hug, turkey trot, and grizzly bear, but discreetly leave out one called the nigger wiggle, named as if Black people were just one more kind of amusing animal. (This dance entailed, for the record, a couple putting their hips against each other's and holding each other's rear ends.)

One of the cutest things about the marvelous television

confection *Crazy Ex-Girlfriend* was that a central character was an Asian guy named Josh, while another character also happened to be named Josh and was always called "White Josh," even to his face, with no one caring. But way back when, it was just as ordinary to call a white Mike of swarthy complexion "Nigger Mike," as in the nickname of a cabaret owner whose establishment helped set Irving Berlin on his way in the aughts. That name made it into his obituaries.

Not long afterward, William Jennings Bryan, iconic populist orator famous for his "Cross of Gold" speech, running for president three times, and depicted onstage and on screen in *Inherit the Wind* by countless august actors, in real life remarked upon Haitians, "Dear me, think of it, Niggers speaking French." Meanwhile, the marine in charge of Haiti on the behalf of our great nation at the time, L. W. T. Waller, made sure all knew that whatever their linguistic aptitudes, the Haitians were "real nigs beneath the surface."

Sometimes the terminology varied. Melville Herskovits was a pioneering anthropologist of what in his time were called Afro American cultures. He did fieldwork in Haiti and among the descendants of escaped slaves in the rain forest of Surinam. He documented the African contribution to the cultures of these and other African-descended peoples. He advocated for the independence of African nations. He was what would today be termed a highly "woke" academic. And, in 1923 in a letter to Margaret Mead, he referred to the people he had been researching as "coons."

Neither Fish nor Fowl: *Nigra* and Other Feints

There was a transitional period between the breeziness of "real nigs beneath the surface" and the cancellation of Paula Deen. Into the twentieth century, with Black figures of authority long past slavery insisting that Black Americans be treated with dignity especially after serving in the First World War, *nigger* began a move from neutral to impolite. But not yet *profane*.

Film is, as always, illuminating. We have been told that early talkies were splendidly vulgar because Barbara Stanwyck openly sleeps her way to the top in *Baby Face*, etc. But linguistically, these films are post-Victorian. Stanwyck's character never says *fuck*, *ass*, or *shit* as the real-life version would have, and in films of this genre, that reticence includes *nigger*. It is, despite the heartless racism of the era, absent in American cinema until the 1960s to my knowledge, other than Gregory Peck including it in a disapproving list of slurs in *Gentleman's Agreement* in 1947. We can only glean it in the shadows.

In the *Gone with the Wind* film no one says it, but in the bestselling book it was based on, Scarlett O'Hara hauls off with: "You're a fool nigger, and the worst day's work Pa ever did was to buy you." She then thinks, "I've said 'nigger' and Mother wouldn't like that at all." There was a veil coming down, such that one was supposed to be polite—approximately in the book, conclusively in the movie. But still, it was always *just* under the same surface that our marine saw "nig"-ness through.

Same period, 1937: a Looney Tunes cartoon (*Porky's Railroad*) has Porky Pig at the helm of a runaway train, which zooms past a pile of logs and blows them away to reveal a perplexed Black man sitting there. We might wonder why this person had been sitting under a pile of logs. This was a joke referring to the expression "nigger in the woodpile," an elderly equivalent to "the elephant in the room." No Looney Tunes character ever says *nigger*, but this joke reveals that their creators were familiar with the word being used with casual humor.

As late as 1966, when I was toddling around my mother in a park in a very "progressive" neighborhood in Philadelphia, an elderly white woman said to her friend at full volume, "Look at the little pickaninny!" Remember, this wasn't Alabama but the City of Brotherly Love, far north of the Mason–Dixon Line. These women had been minted in the era of "Nigger Mike," and we can reasonably assume that their relationship to *nigger* was comfortable to an extent that probably embarrassed their grandchildren.

In fact, had they been Southerners, they would likely have been given to a term that neatly symbolized the stage between casual and condemned: *nigra*, with the dignified *Negro* somehow too far a stretch, leaving a new term just different enough from *nigger* to pass as civilized.

Even into the 1970s, the word's usage in the media was different than it is today. *The Jeffersons*, portraying a Black family who move from working-class Queens to affluence in a Manhattan apartment tower, was considered a brash, modern, and even thoughtful statement at the time. Here was the era when television shows took a jump into a previously unknown realism. The contrast between the goofy vaudeville of *Here's Lucy* and the salty shout-fests on *The Jeffersons* was as stark as that between *Blondie* and *The Boondocks*. So even though there was no such thing as a joke about *pussy* on an American television show in the way British shows could get past with, it was almost a defining element of a show like *The Jeffersons* that loud-mouthed, streety George would use *nigger* to refer to Black people with (and without) affection.

In fact, George freely used it in an early episode while playing the Dozens ("Take it easy, nigga, wolfin' at my door / With your yellow behind I'm gonna mop up the entire floor!"). On the show the character began in, *All in the Family*, while bigoted Archie Bunker did not say the word as his real-life counterpart would have, George did, such as raging about the possibility of having (white) Edith Bunker help out at his dry cleaner's ("The niggers will think she owns the store and the honkies will think we bleached the help!"). Even Isabel Sanford's Louise got in a solid "Nigga, please!" in one episode, appalled at the high cost of a watch.

Nor were Black characters the only ones to say it; the writers aired the "real" *nigger* as well. White men used it no fewer than four times on an episode where George meets modern Klansmen. But whites weren't limited to it only in "very special episode" cases like this. George called white neighbor Tom Willis "honky" and Tom petulantly fires back, "How would you like it if I called you nigger?" I saw it at the time and it sounded perfectly okay—after all, he was just talking *about* it, not using it. But today, it would be considered beyond the pale (so to speak!) to have Willis use the word even just to refer to it.

From Tacky to Taboo

That outright forbidden status of *nigger* settled in only at the end of the twentieth century. 2002 was about the last year that a mainstream publisher would allow a book to be titled *Nigger* as Randall Kennedy's was—as I write this, only eighteen years later, the notion of publishing something with that title sounds like science fiction. In fact, only a year afterward, a medical school employee at the University of Virginia said, "I can't believe in this day and age that there's a sports team in our nation's capital named the Redskins. That is as derogatory to Indians as having a team called Niggers would be to Blacks." NAACP head Julian Bond suggested this person undergo mandatory sensitivity training, saying that his gut instinct was that the person deserved to be fired. The idea, then, was that the word was unutterable regardless of context; today, that employee would likely only whisper or mime it, or use the N-word nickname.

Sitcoms of the twenty-first century steer clear except under the most pressing conditions, if even that. There's a 2007 episode of *South Park* ("With Apologies to Jesse Jackson") in which the word is used several dozen times. However, the creators took heat even for that, and the crucial fact is that *South Park* is a cartoon, full of characters rendered as cute construction-paper cutouts with squeaky voices. Note how unthinkable it is to imagine the word used that freely with live actors, even tongue-in-cheek, and even on clever, layered shows such as *Arrested Development*, or ones with multiracial casts such as *Brooklyn Nine-Nine*.

Rather, the modern American uses "the N-word" instead. This tradition settled in after the O. J. Simpson trial, when detective Mark Fuhrman became famous for having used the full word in the past. Black prosecutor Christopher Darden refused to utter it, and with the high profile of the case, and in seemingly saluting Allen Walker Read's take in deigning *nigger* "the filthiest, dirtiest, nastiest word in the English language," he brought on a new era.

That was in early 1995, and in the fall of that year I did a sober radio interview about the word in which I and the guests freely used it, with nary a bleep. That had been normal until then, but would not be for much longer, such that the interview is now a period piece.

Transitioning to the "N-word" euphemism in the late 1990s, it's safe to say no one was thinking about the linguistic coarseness of an LA detective or something a not especially charismatic prosecutor said one day during a monthslong trial.

Rather, Darden's reticence was a symptom of something already in the air: the larger shift in sensibility that rendered slurs the new profanity.

This occurred as Generation X, born from about 1965 to 1980, came of age. These were the first Americans raised in the post–civil rights era. To Generation X, legalized segregation was a bygone barbarism, and overt racist attitudes were ridiculed and socially punished in general society. Racism continued to exist, of course, in endless manifestations, but it became "complicated"—something to hide, to dissemble about, and among at least an enlightened cohort, something to check oneself for and call out in others, to a degree unknown in perhaps any society until then.

The Norman Lear sitcoms such as *The Jeffersons, All in the Family,* and *Maude* brightly reflected this sea change. *Mr. Ed* premiered in 1961 but would have made perfect sense (and maybe more sense) to audiences of 1951. *Cheers* premiered in 1981 but would have fit in with little adjustment into television of 1971. *All in the Family* premiered in 1971, but in its pitiless ridicule of Archie Bunker's bigotry and George hauling off with *nigger,* would have seemed like a projection from Mars to audiences of 1961.

For Americans of this post-countercultural cohort, the pox on matters of God and the body seemed quaint beyond discussion, while a pox on matters of slurring groups seemed urgent beyond discussion. The N-word euphemism was an organic outcome.

Nigger, Please?

My treatment of *nigger* so far as simply a "slur" will seem incomplete given the fuller reality of its usage in American English. One may sense a shoe that has yet to drop—what about how Black people use the word with one another?

I refer, of course, to what is termed the *appropriation* of the term of abuse into one of affection. One thinks also of the similar use of *faggot* among gay men, and *bitch* among women. Less known is that this kind of appropriation occurs widely. It is a tendency among humans to treat slurs directed against them as equivalents to "buddy." This represents a warm reality among people. Hierarchy is inimical to intimacy; affection entails a degree of leveling, diminishment even. The Black man who calls his friend "nigger" is saying, "Hey, man, there are people who would call you that the same way they would call me that, and yet we know despite our susceptibility to that abuse and denigration that we're okay. In fact, to the extent that whites think of 'niggers' as a nuisance, it's a kind of power we have."

It's never that explicit, naturally, but this is all about being a social creature. As such, while in Russian the dictionary definition of *muzhik* is (lowly) peasant, it can be used to mean "good fella." It expresses the Russian *On s nami!*—"He's one of us!" The French *mec* for "guy" has a contested etymology, but the main choices for origin are "cigarette butt," "criminal awaiting trial," or "pimp"—enough said. A *Seinfeld* episode nailed the phenomenon among white men with George gleefully joining in with a boozy bunch of guys calling one another "bastard." Here, also, the *bastard* could have been a network-standards version of the saltier *son of a bitch* that was common among the same kinds of men before about 1960.

In that vein, another historical use of *nigger* would be as confounding to us as *cock* referring to a vagina. In the early 1800s, Native Americans, Mexicans, and even white men in the mountain fur trade in the western United States were referred to in folksy fashion as "niggurs." They actually referred to themselves that way—"Well, that was the time this niggur first felt like taking to the mountains," a white "mountain man" is quoted as saying in 1825. Odd, or the same old thing: human humility can mean applying to yourself a nasty epithet, whether or not it originally was applied to your kind.

Indeed, to term this "appropriation" sanitizes the business. It leaves out an intermediate point between *nigger* as slur and *nigger* as "buddy"—a certain element of self-hate, or at least intragroup discrimination. It would be disingenuous to pretend that a closer look at its use among Black people does not entail an idea that only "bad" Black people are the "niggers." Comedian Chris Rock only set down in the public glare what Black people have long known, that *nigger* can mean not just "pal" but "Black person who holds us back."

Who's more racist: black people or white people? Black people. You know why? Because black people hate black people,

> *too. Everything white people don't like about black people,*
> *black people don't like about black people.... Every time*
> *black people want to have a good time, niggers mess it up....*
> *Can't keep a disco open more than three weeks. Grand open-*
> *ing? Grand closing. Can't go to a movie the first week it*
> *opens. Why? Because niggers are shooting at the screen.*

That was "just" a comedy routine, but there's a reason why it resonated, putting Rock on the map as more than just another comic. George Jefferson's remark about how "the niggers will think she owns the store" was similarly a dig, as was any usage of the word in the abusive atmosphere of the Dozens.

Before ragtime and jazz became America's classical music, Black people of the middle class and above were often as horrified as others by their origins in illicit milieus and their invitation to premarital intimacies. Will Marion Cook was a Black violinist who with the 1898 hit *Clorindy* ushered the ragtime sound onto Broadway and made American theater music "hot." Yet when his very "proper" Washington, DC, Black bourgeois mother heard her son reveling in that kind of music, her response was "I've sent you all over the world to study and become a great musician and you return such a nigger!"

And going that far back is important: the Black usage of *nigger* in all of its auras is a product neither of the recent "inner city" street nor of hip-hop music or culture. One needs not isolated once-removed citations from white authors like Mark Twain to know—we can read it in the speech of Black people themselves. In a precious legacy of the Great Depression, in the 1930s the Works Progress Administration assigned writers and students to fan out across the South and beyond to interview ex-slaves about their lives. In thousands of interviews we see (and in the case of a few dozen recordings, hear) people who had lived as slaves having their say.

What we see is that these interview subjects use *nigger* in contempt, affection, and all shades in between. It is, for better or for worse, often their default term for a Black person. Andy Anderson of Texas, ninety-four years old and thus someone who learned to speak when John Tyler was president, casually says, "Massa Haley owned my folks and 'bout twelve other families of niggers.... There am 'bout thirty old and young niggers and 'bout twenty piccaninnies..." Silvia King, also of Texas and very old at the time, fondly recalled, "De smokehouse am full of bacon sides and cure hams and barrels lard and 'lasses. When a nigger want to eat, he jes' ask and git the passel," and of a man assigned to her as husband, "I don't bother with dat nigger's name much, he jes' Bob to me."

It is no surprise, then, that *nigger* as a term of in-group identification in all of its resonances decorates most of the famous works of the Harlem Renaissance by figures such as Zora Neale Hurston and Claude McKay. *Big Nigger* was what Hurston almost named her novel *Jonah's Gourd Vine*, and meant it as (essentially) a compliment to the character based on her wayward father. McKay's hit novel *Home to Harlem* of 1928 channels Chris Rock with proclamations by Black migrants from the South such as "You nevah know when niggers am gwineta git crazy-mad," but then smiles with lines such as "One thing I know is niggers am made foh life." The word was common coin in Black "toast" oral poetry, where *nigger* connoted "badass," as in the signature "Stagolee" (as in Stagger Lee) routine depicting this hero as "the baddest nigger that ever lived," a "bad nigger off the block and didn't take shit from nobody."

A generation after McKay's book, Claude Brown's magnificent portrait of Black life in Harlem, *Manchild in the Promised Land*, also showed how the word was used then (and now):

> *You're one of these complacent niggers out here who managed to get by and not have it bother them directly . . . when the shit comes down on you, you're going to be one of the angriest niggers out here on this street, man . . . you see all these niggers running out here talking about they want some white girl. Damn, I don't want me nothin' but a nigger woman.*

Note the toggling in this one passage between contempt ("complacent niggers"), Stagolee pride ("angriest niggers"), indifference ("all these niggers"), and sincere affection ("I don't want me nothin' but a nigger woman"). This is a dazzling demonstration of what a word can mean in this captious thing called real language.

I recall a Black American intellectual superstar in 2002 referring to another one as "one of those a-gayn and a-gayn niggers," mocking this other scholar's pronunciation as suggesting a certain pretension. I will take to my grave whom the two were but must note that the "a-gayn" person in question (who is, for the record, not me) does not, in fact, pronounce the word that way. No matter—the charge contained a deft combination of dissing and respect.

Alternate terms to *nigger* were equally revealing back in the day. We must bring Will Marion Cook back in. *Clorindy* included lyrics such as "Warm coons a' prancin' / Swell coons a' dancin' / Tough coons who'll want to fight." Our justifiable impulse is to assume that Cook, along with poet lyricist Paul Laurence Dunbar, were catering to the requirements of white audiences. Cook, a stridently and even insufferably proud soul, never said anything to indicate such, and to the extent that at the time Black men were rarely sought out to say how they *really* felt, we can glean more from how his peers did. They teach us that men like Cook and Dunbar had the same multifarious take on *coon* that so many Black people today have on *nigger*. Sylvester Russell was drama critic at a leading Black newspaper of the era, the *Indianapolis Freeman*. He was hardly a Pollyannaish sort who thought Black people needed to sit tight and be polite and whites would come to like them. He staged a sit-in sixty years before cameras would start recording such incidents and make a louder case for racial justice to his country. He disapproved of *nigger* in all facets, yet he solemnly opined in 1904 that "the Negro race has no objections to the word 'coon.'" *What?* But then even today, the warm term for best friend *ace boon coon* is still remembered by Black people of a certain age and then some.

In 1905, Russell interviewed Black stage composer and performer Bob Cole—the Lin-Manuel Miranda of the era, creating a series of all-Black Broadway shows during the Theodore Roosevelt administration when American theater was otherwise pitilessly #SoWhite. Cole, for one, couldn't abide *coon*—"The word 'coon' is very insinuating and must soon be eliminated"—but he had no problem with *darkey*.

Appropriation is a very old story.

How Come They Can Use It?

As a linguist who dedicates himself to sharing linguistics with the public and who is also Black and has written on Black English, I am often asked whether I "approve" of the appropriation of *nigger* by Black people. I do—blunt the sting by throwing it back, I say. But what gets lost in a pithy reply is that words are not granitic units that only mean one thing, and this applies not only to obviously unrelated soundalikes like *pen* as a writing tool and *pen* as a corral. The rub is when one meaning develops from another but drifts just far enough to straddle the boundary between alternate meaning and new word altogether. Think of *combination*. You know what it means—"when stuff is put together." But it means more than that. The number you use to open a lock is a combination (i.e., of numbers, but we don't think of that consciously). Or, in the nineteenth century, that which we know as a labor union was called a "combination." Usually we don't have trouble with words meaning two very different things. *Nigger* has been appropriated, to be sure—but the old meaning persists alongside, and isn't going away any more than we will be letting go of using *combination* to mean a combining despite working with locks. What my questioner means is whether appropriating is corrective; the answer is no. Appropriation will just yield a second meaning coexisting with the earlier one. In the same way, women may use *bitch* affectionately, but men can still use it to wound.

With *nigger*, what makes the issue especially challenging is that the people who appropriated it have a speech pattern different from the standard as their in-group code. This is not true with the appropriation of *faggot* and *bitch*. Black English is English but with slightly distinct sound patterns. One of them is that *r*'s at the end of syllables are elided—this is true not only of our one word but across the board: "Mo' money," etc. There is nothing uniquely "Black" about that—*r*'s are mushy as consonants go (compare them to the clickiness of *p*, *t*, or *k*) and at the ends of syllables they have a way of fading. Queen Elizabeth, a Boston Southie resident, and Paul Hogan all say something like "staw" for *store*. Black Americans do, too, likely encouraged in it by the fact that most of the African languages spoken by slaves liked their syllables ending in vowels rather than sharp, officious consonants. Think Kunta Kinte from *Roots* or the *Lion King*'s "*hakuna matata.*"*

Hence: after a questioner brings up the appropriation issue in a public forum, often another one, usually a young Black one, carefully notes the difference between *nigger*—the slur—and *nigga*—the term of affection. This is because an integral part of being casual is using the casual speech style, if it is part of one's repertoire. Thus it comes out in the wash that usually, when a Black person says *nigger* casually, they render it as *nigga*, which leaves the *nigger* pronunciation sounding alien, as the way white people say it. The result is a hazy popular sense that *nigga* is different from *nigger*, but with the genuflective overlay, conditioned by print as well as propriety, that both the white person calling someone a *nigger* and the Black person giving props to his *nigga* are using "the same word."

This is subtle stuff. In Scots, the way the word *home* comes out is *hame*. Scots is, most would allow, a kind of English, and Scottish people who speak Scots also speak "English" English and are familiar with the word *home*. It's just that *hame* is what you say as your "Scots self," referring to something more specific, your comfort zone, what Scandis call *hygge*, and what

---

*No slaves—or vanishingly few—brought to America spoke Swahili, despite that language's having been chosen for pragmatic reasons as Black Americans' "mother" language in the late 1960s. A great many instead spoke languages related to Swahili in the same way as French is related to Spanish, such as Kikongo, where words were similarly inclined to end in vowels.

Black Americans refer to as "up" something. "We're partying here up in the house" someone says from the ground floor—using "up" as marker as the in-group warmth of the gathering. So, *hame* is not simply "the way you pronounce *home* in Scots." One doesn't say "The package was sent to his hame instead of to his office" or refer to the *hameless*—in cases like those, Scots use the "English" English word *home* alongside *hame*. Rather, *home* birthed *hame*. There's a relationship, and maybe even an umbilical cord—but *hame* is its own thing.

Nigga is similar. Louise Jefferson didn't say "Nigger, please!"—she said "Nigga, please!" On the magisterially insightful sitcom *30 Rock*, when the starchy Black "Twofer" character says the word, even the whites hear it as hurtful. Demeanor is only part of the problem; more directly, it's that he says *nigger*, which conditions a different emotional reaction in people of all kinds, and refers to something else altogether. That is, it's a different word.

A Funeral for the N-Word?

On race issues, it is important to attend to the past as well as the present: a part of sophistication is to understand that the past leaves legacies. As such, many feel that *nigger* should be banned in all of its renditions, including Black people calling one another *nigga*. Claims such as mine that *nigga* is actually a new word, a product of something as abstract and faceless as language change, can seem tinny. It seems to frame an issue of sociohistorical and emotional urgency as if it were a mere matter of textbook nerdery.

There are Black people who call for *everyone* to stop using it, rejecting it as too polluted by its origins to be treated as anything truly separate. However, any quest to end, or even significantly lessen, the usage of *nigga* as opposed to *nigger* is so unlikely of success that there is an argument for changing our lens. These objectors are up against an implacable reality: the incessant frequency with which millions of Black people use it *and always have*, and most of the time with so powerful a bonding power, redolent of leveling and warmth—humanity, in other words. History is littered with the husks of initiatives to change how our day-to-day language is used—i.e., of just about all of them. The chance that calls to bury the N-word's use as a term of endearment will have any effect is likely none, and anyone with any doubts about the matter need only listen to the real-life usage among a great many Black people. The horse is out of the barn.

In fact, I must push a bit more: in modern Black English parlance, *nigga* has penetrated so deeply as to even be used to refer to animals. A real statement: *My cat fell in the toilet, damn that nigga dumb.* Or a sentence I love almost as much as the one about English lacking gender except for words like *waitress*, *cock*, and *bitch*: *A wasp just stung me on some drive-by type shit, nigga just stung me and bounced.* The word has drilled so far down that it almost means "it." Here to stay, I'm afraid.

In the meantime, however, non-Black people who feel that it is unfair that only Black people are allowed to use it might adopt a more scientific approach to language. Just as we develop our palates by trying a wider range of foods, or enjoy an illuminating course on classical music, an empirical take on language reveals a much richer and messier correspondence between words and meanings than the tidiness of the dictionary suggests. We especially must understand that a word can develop a new meaning while the old one persists alongside.

From *acute* as meaning smart, the word *cute* developed, and for a good while could mean either "smart" or "good-looking." Imagine if *combination* had drifted into common usage as a word for "sex" in the way that *intercourse* has instead. As in, *the pair was apprehended in combination upon which the vice squad promptly*... Now imagine certain people deciding that the word *combination* was thus improper for "mixed company." Would it then make sense to bridle when someone used *combination* in reference to padlocks? Victorians could have easily embraced such a doily nicety, but we see ourselves as vastly more enlightened.

"But this is *race* we're talking about!" some will understandably object, and where we go from there is a judgment call. (The Victorian, it must be said, would have grumbled, "But this is *sex* we're talking about!" sensing it as just as much of a mic drop. In his defense, opinions still differ on whether *that sucks* counts as vulgar because of its easily recoverable original connotation.) But on the N-word, one thing urging what we might call a more liberal verdict, allowing that a viciously abusive word has birthed, of all things, a term of love, is if we insist that *nigger* and *nigga* are one and the same, even Black people can be accused of using the slur rather than the term of endearment.

Nothing could have put a sillier point on it than when in 2019 a Black high school security guard in Madison, Wisconsin, was fired when a misbehaving Black student repeatedly called him the N-word and he retorted, "Do not call me nigga!" The people firing him were operating under a policy of "no exceptions" regarding this most profane of profanities, but the two were saying varieties of *nigga*, not *nigger*. To the extent that the people who fired this man seem Victorian themselves—including in their insensitivity to nuances of race and language—we might consider the episode evidence that there are two N-words, and that one of them is, even in its more sour shades, permissible speech.

Okay, but Can *They* Use It?

We still aren't out of the woods, because even if we accept that there are two N-words and get past thinking that Black men are saying *nigger*, what do we do with white guys thinking they're saying *nigga*?

It can be odd to hear Latino men doing it, but then they are what we classify as "of color" and often live alongside and among Black Americans. Hearing Asian American people use it takes a little more adjustment. Even then, though, we think not to overgeneralize. Why wouldn't some Asian American men growing up in non-white communities, going to school alongside people speaking Black English, and listening to the same hip-hop, not start calling one another *nigga*? And after all, they, too, are "of color."

Ah, but when we turn to white guys, none of this works. Even if the men in question are from struggling communities, they are of the race that originated the slur version. Still, it isn't hard to hear white men under a certain age jocularly calling one another *nigga*, of all things, as a term of fellowship, and many are hardly from the hood—I've caught it used by ones at certain prestigious universities. A time traveler from as recently as 1960 would find this as odd as we would find respectable medieval men introducing themselves as Fuckbythenavel.

If it's all about leveling, then this white usage of *nigga* can sound especially revolting. Is the idea that to humble someone, even if in affection, it's particularly effective to call him a Black person? But I suspect this analysis is a little facile. The white men who use the word this way have grown up in post-1990s America, where hip-hop is less Black music than mainstream music, played at weddings and common knowledge among even the most Wonder Bread of teens. They have grown up with *nigga* played endlessly and in all its facets directly into their ears, by artists they cherish for the same reason we all cherish our favorite ones. That is, they hear themselves in this music— the rhythm, the swagger, the sneer, the joy, the dance moves, the sense of camaraderie, the *anti-whiteness*... and *so*, the question would be: Why would they not start to feel comfortable calling one another *nigga*?

To them, the word has the redolence of gingerbread fresh out of the oven (with weed in it, maybe)—not of some old-time Southern bigot. Adoring and thus adopting the poses of hip-hop—and personality and identity are, to such a degree, performance—they on a certain level want to *be* a Black person. Talk to them about this and time how quickly it takes for them to say so, or at least start to and then walk it back.

Yes, they may miss that being a Black person has serious downsides obscured by hip-hop's wordplay and beats and imagery and legend. That ignorance is naive, but different from contempt. Meanwhile, the cultural "browning" of America since the mid-1990s means that a generation of white people has grown up so immersed in Black music that they manage the equipoise of being "woke" about racism while also sensing the music as part of themselves. *Nigga* is as integral to that music as *sweetheart*, *darling*, and *baby* were to the pop of another era. This means that the N-word has taken on yet another facet.

Make no mistake—whites have taken grisly advantage of the subtleties involved. In 2005, in Queens, New York, white Nicholas Minucci chased down Glenn Moore, a Black man, shouting "nigger" at him as he eventually beat him in the head with an aluminum bat. Minucci tried to defend himself with the notion that he, as a resident of a multiethnic neighborhood, had been using the term of endearment, as in shouting, "Hey, man!" (and then beating him in the head...). Especially choice was that at trial, Minucci made a show of carrying a copy of Randall Kennedy's book on the word, which had been widely discussed in the few years before.

We must consider whether the Minucci case should motivate banning the white usage not just of *nigger* but of *nigga*—if we allow that there is a difference—out of wariness of such excrescences. But how often do white men address Black—as opposed to other white—men as *nigga*? I'm sure there are interracial groups in which white guys call their Black friends *nigga* and no one minds, although they'd be horrified to find video of the evidence on YouTube. ("People wouldn't understand!")

All of this can start to feel like science fiction, as if someone asked when it will be okay to do a white production of *Raisin in the Sun* if there can be an all-Black version of *Cat on a Hot Tin Roof.* Just as a white Bigger Thomas, even if done to a turn by Edward Norton or Brad Pitt, is unthinkable, we might say that the white usage of *nigga* is just beyond contempt, no questions asked. Too soon, maybe. Or, just never?

Consider, though, that there is mirror effect, all very *The Lady from Shanghai*, as the evolution goes even further. Not only are white men calling one another *nigga*, but Black men are referring to non-Black men as *nigga* in a sense that means basically "guy." *There's this white nigga in my class who...* one can find in tweets and beyond. Asian people can be *nigga*. This word has legs.

It puts me in an awkward position. The linguist does not judge. The thinker on race, however, does. And quite honestly, when I hear white men bouncing down the street calling one another *nigga*, I get it. It would have happened sooner or later. They are using a word different from *nigger*. They wish we would understand—and I will admit: I do. I'd rather they kept it on the private side, and there are various ways that they might and likely could reveal racist bias, but that linguistic usage is not one of them. It just sounds like it, because language change affects all words, knowing no distinctions of respectability or taboo, and too ineluctably for either racism or moral discomfort to hold back.

Opinions, of course, will differ.

Who Knew It Was a Pronoun?

So permissive, I know. But partly because, as we have seen before, when language change reaches up and grabs profanity into its churn, often it creates not just new words but new grammar. *Nigger* is no exception, and we should close this rather gloomy, touchy chapter with something fun. English likes turning cusses into pronouns, such as *his ass* for *him* and *my shit* for *myself.* Less obvious is that in the way Black English is spoken, even *nigger* has gone pronominal!

Here's how.

A nigga haven't made myself breakfast yet.

Ever since a nigga taught myself how to roll, I've smoked every day.

In these sentences, spoken by actual people, *a nigga* is linked to *myself*, in a way that shows that in straight-up unmonitored modern Black English, *a nigga* means just "I." In the first sentence, the meaning isn't that some stray offstage "nigga" hasn't made this person breakfast yet, but that *he himself* hasn't. The *haven't* there, in the old-school grammar sense, agrees properly with *I* rather than *he*—it isn't *A nigga hasn't* as in "That negro hath not." It's the same with *A nigga haven't had doughnuts for months, I ain't livin' right.* I *haven't*, but he *hasn't*—and "a nigga" *haven't*.

Obviously this is not the only way that Black people, or even some Black people, say *I*. Rather, this *I* has a certain self-skeptical flavor—I'm too lazy to make myself breakfast; I'm not good enough to myself to treat myself to Dunkin' Donuts enough; I'm a pothead. This is a dismissive pronoun, like *my ass*.

It's one of those things that happened step by step, tiny changes piling up like in a game of telephone until the output is stunningly unlike the input. *What in hell is this?* becomes *What the hell is this?* which conditions *the hell* to branch off to be used in phrases like *the hell with it* and *the hell I will*, in which *hell* makes no blessed sense. In Black English, one can say, "Come on, help a nigga out," to ask for help in a pleading kind of way, usually to another Black person, calling upon their sense of group fellowship by referring to oneself in a self-effacing way.

But what you mean is "Help *me* out." There is a short step from there to using *a nigga* to mean *I* and *me*.

Further, many uses of *nigga* in the third person qualify almost as pronouns, based on the same criteria that make up the *ass* and *shit* paradigms. *Nigga can't even stand up straight*—the temptation is to suppose that this is "short for" *Yon nigger cannot even stand up straight*. But the two don't mean the same thing. The one with *nigger* is too harsh. *The nigga* is warmer, but the profane callout is more explicit than when you say just *Nigga can't even stand up straight*. In this latter version, the flavor of *nigga* is intended merely as a pinch of salt, and *nigga* is pronounced with no accent—just like a pronoun. "Nigga can't even stand up straight" as in "He can't even stand up straight." There is grammatical machinery involved here. When this new third-person pronoun is used as an object, one needs to append *the*. One does not say *Just tell nigga!* One must phrase it as *Just tell the nigga!*, which means not "Do inform that Negro," but "Just tell him." "Just tell him." "Just tell the nigga."

The exquisite sentence about the wasp on page 197 takes this even further. Only a naughty, I-don't-give-a-fuck quality renders the wasp a "nigger," one presumes, as in "ba-ad nigger" à la Richard Pryor and Shaft. But this sentence takes the word so far from the Old South that it barely qualifies as rational unless we class it, again, as a pronoun. A dismissive one, but pronoun all the same. Then *niggaz* in the plural is used in the same way—*Niggaz thought they had fooled me but I showed up anyway*. Here, *niggaz* is a flava-ful *they*.

This means that we must flesh out even further our real-life depiction of how pronouns work in American usage. Black English includes some additional dismissive pronouns. In the third person, *nigga* is not usually used for women, and thus:

NEUTRAL DISMISSIVE	BLACK	REFLEXIVE	INTIMATE DISMISSIVE	REFLEXIVE
I / me	my ass	a nigga	myself	my shit
you	your ass		yourself	your shit
he / him	his ass	(the) nigga	himself	his shit
she / her	her ass		herself	her shit
it	that shit	(the) nigga	itself	
we / us	our asses		ourselves	our shit
y'all	your asses		yourselves	your shit
they / them	their asses	(the) niggaz	themselves	their shit

It's Not Funny. But It's Glorious.

It must be clear that this chart is not meant in fun. The way we are presented with English in grammar books is as subtractive as an old etiquette guide to dating, as if no one had sex except with the benefit of clergy until the pill. The grammarian understands that we distinguish objects from subjects with *me* versus *I*, and get a little further into reality in documenting that we also attend to matters of formality with differences like *tú* versus *usted* in Spanish for *you*.

However, conventional grammar treats as garnish equally central aspects of how we express ourselves in the true, roiling realm of sociality that language is designed to maneuver us through. Familiarity and warmth are as key to self-expression as case marking, even if they feel less faceless and clinical. This means that a person wangling the difference between *me* and *my ass* and *my shit* and even *a nigga* is dwelling in complexity, of all things, as deftly as French people using their subjunctive mood. Stand in line at a post office, or watch a movie by Martin Scorsese or a television show like *Succession*, or listen to hip-hop, and you are hearing the wondrous thing of American English "in the wild."

The real story of *nigger* is here. A person spontaneously controlling the difference between what *nigger* and *nigga* mean, and when to use each and how, is working a kind of magic, including hearing that a character like *30 Rock*'s Twofer (or me!)*

---

*"Yeah, I use it!" a prominent Black public intellectual at our joint event once said, to the delight of the audience. Do I? As will likely not surprise you, no—I am not given to addressing Black men I like as "my nigga." I believe I only used *nigga* in that way once, and it was less affectionate than "in-group abasement." When I was about twelve, a rowdy Black peer was given to intimidating people into giving him their stuff. One day he tried to take my bike from me—not to use but to keep. He was fond of using our little word as part of his shtick. I have socked someone and not been hit back exactly two times in my life. The first time I have always been ashamed of and will keep to myself. But this second time, something jumped up in me and I said, "Nigga, you *must* be kidding!" and socked that little, well… on his head and he (much to my surprise) hit the ground and skulked off. Truth to tell, I doubt I said the word right. But I kept my damned bike!

may not work the word in quite the right way. *Nigger* is not just "a slur." It is profanity, and profanity of a dazzling range of shades, in a way that reveals it, in all of its menace, filth, scorn, teasing, warmth, love, and interracial outreach, as one of English's words most—of all things—marvelous.

7

THE OTHER
F-WORD

For those disinclined to classify the word featured in the previous chapter as profanity, *faggot* may seem even more of a stretch—distinct from profanity, a *slur*, but hardly akin to the taboo words familiar to the anthropologist.

That view has its merits, but fewer and fewer as time goes on. As with *nigger*, the way Americans feel about *faggot* has changed considerably over the past few decades. A then-versus-now comparison reveals the difference between slur and profanity.

In 1987, Eddie Murphy's stand-up film *Raw* liberally included references, alternately affectionate and dismissive, of "faggots." Today, that would never get by in a mainstream presentation, even as we have become used to acclaimed shows like

Girls regularly showing full-frontal nudity and sexual acts, and using all the words we have discussed (except, pointedly, the one treated in the previous chapter).

Rather, in 2007 when Isaiah Washington, famous as a central character on *Grey's Anatomy*, called a fellow cast member a faggot during rehearsals, he was fired from the show and his career suffered massively. Washington had not helped matters by using the word again when referring to it, in trying to defend himself. The parallel with the new rules on *nigger* are clear. Washington, who is Black, as it happened, was as caught short on how this other word is now taboo rather than just mean as the woman comparing the Redskins to a hypothetical team "Niggers" had been. He would be unlikely to make the mistake today.

Equally indicative of the sea change was when that same year, notoriously provocative conservative commentator Ann Coulter said of presidential candidate John Edwards: "I was going to have a few comments on the other Democratic presidential candidate, John Edwards, but it turns out that you have to go into rehab if you use the word 'faggot,' so I'm—so, kind of at an impasse, can't really talk about Edwards, so I think I'll just conclude here and take your questions."

Coulter was referring to the Isaiah Washington episode, and the conservative audience at the event applauded. However, she was lambasted not only by the Gay and Lesbian Alliance Against Defamation (GLAAD) but also by many Republicans. Editorialist Andrew Sullivan's take, as a gay man, was that Coulter's aiming the word at Edwards was indeed egregious, but that it would have been wiser—and accurate—to call out as PC excess the idea that people like Washington ought submit themselves to formal psychological cleansing. Today, even that opinion would be condemned from left-of-center and beyond as roundly as Coulter's statement was. *Faggot* is no longer just a slur—it has become, since the days of Eddie Murphy using it casually in a comedy routine shown nationwide, profane. One is not to utter it, period, no questions asked.

A Bundle of Sticks?

For a word used to refer disparagingly to homosexual men, *faggot* has the strangest history of any other in this book. So strange that the basics get around a fair amount—it's a common factoid on the vine that the word originally referred to, of all things, a bundle of sticks.

It may seem odd that there would ever have *been* a word for a bundle of sticks at all. We must put ourselves in the frame of mind of medieval Europeans for whom fire and the burning of wood were as central to existence as the internet is to us. Kindling was often handled in bound bundles rather than clattering armfuls of loose sticks and branches, and the bundles were a staple of existence such that the first attestation of the word— which appears in Scottish just as early instances of *fuck*—is in a list of someone's effects after death, in 1312.

Thereafter the word appears regularly in documents of all

kinds, with an inevitably peculiar effect. "The Black Prince," litterateur Joseph Addison informed us in 1711 in his daily magazine, "filled a Ditch with Faggots as successfully as the Generals of our times do it with Fascines." A fascine is a type of faggot, longer and made of brushwood and used to fortify or provide paths. The reader in Addison's time knew the difference.

Because faggots of wood kept a fire going, the word was extended metaphorically to being burnt at the stake. A man was described in 1563 as "Running out of Germanye for feare of the fagot" while in 1631 someone grimly enumerated grisly ways of being executed: "the wheele, greediron, racke and faggot." This was hardly the only extended usage. The word was so familiar that it sprouted a lovely plethora of meanings. Few things about language would more stun today's American time traveler than to experience eighteenth- and nineteenth-century English as largely approachable, only to occasionally hear people casually referring to "faggots" of assorted kinds.

It needed not be a big, clumsy clattering thing. To ingratiate oneself, one could come bearing "a little Faggot of Thyme, Savory, and Parsley." It did not have to even involve sticks or plants. Ralph Waldo Emerson noted in 1854 that "the psalms and liturgies of churches are a fagot of selections gathered through ages." It could even be abstract. Horace Walpole in 1742 offered a friend "my fagot of compliments." Irish poet Louis MacNeice sneered about people who go about with "a faggot of useless memories."

That last one was as late as 1939, and there was a reason I

noted that the *American* time traveler would be thrown by such usages. *Faggot* as profanity is an American development. Here, we often note the "bundle of sticks" etymology with an assumption that the usage fell into eclipse in the deep past, but in the United Kingdom it has lived on.

The British, for example, eat faggots: a matter of chopped pig meat and crumbs mashed (bundled?) together, wrapped in bacon and rolled into a ball. I describe it clinically as an American, but as I write, there are Brits happily dining on faggots and potatoes. Some of them will then go out to smoke what they call a fag—i.e., cigarette.

Thus over there, the "bundle of sticks" usage has morphed along in ways that more or less make intuitive sense. In other countries this included the name of the instrument called the bassoon, which is a *fagotto* in Italian, *Fagott* in German, etc. The instrument looks like a bundle of sticks though it is not one. In America, however, the word took a series of turns that make sense in themselves, but step by step yielded a result no one could have expected. A faggot as a long, heavy instrument is one thing, as a suety meatball is another—but how in the world did the word get from kindling to gay men?

From Wood to Human

Things like that don't happen all in one flash. Rather, we seek the word coming to refer first just to people of some sort. That did begin across the pond, in reference to conscripting stray men to serve as "dummy" soldiers to make a regiment flagging in actual personnel seem full when officially tallied. "In ancient times, it was not uncommon for a colonel to muster his livery-men, and fill up the blanks with faggots, and then draw pay for a full regiment," an Irish newspaper informs us in 1849. The usage makes more sense than it seems—a comparison of these "dummy" figures with bundles of sticks. A Beaumont and Fletcher play from 1625 got across how the meaning jumped the fence from wood to people when a commander growls, "Tell the great General, my Companies are no fagots to fill breaches." The image compares the illegitimacy and cluelessness of fake recruits to the inertness of the bundles of sticks used to fill ditches.

This set the scene for a general application of *faggot* in the meaning of "worthless person" to go beyond fake soldiers. Per-haps unsurprisingly given the tragedy of human nature, the first target was women. If there was anything peculiar to women that led to this comparison, it may have been the idea that she was a mere bag of bones akin to a bundle of sticks. Hence "She struck at me, she did, the good-for-nothing faggot!" in a novel of 1862. For the record, the faggot in question here is just fifteen years old, against a claim sometimes found that the word applied to older women. Similar is "Rot her, the dirty little faggot, she tor-ments me" in 1796, referring to a woman who we know from the context was of nubile age.

Sometimes the female wasn't even human. I may have found

my third favorite English sentence—after the one about English marking gender with "waitress, cock, bitch, etc." and the one about the wasp where "nigga just stung me and bounced"—in something D. H. Lawrence grumbled in 1925 in reference to a cow: "To me she is fractious, tiresome and a faggot."

Who among us is surprised at the short step from women to children, such that we get on the Isle of Wight in 1886, "Come here, ye young faggot," while down in Hertfordshire, one heard "A pa'cel o' yoong faggots, that's what ye are," recorded in 1948. An Irish man of our times recalls, "I actually remember when we were kids, my mother used to call us 'little faggots.' At one time, it would have been said in the same way someone would go, 'You little brat' or 'You little shit': 'You little faggot, what are you up to?'"

But our point of interest is *faggot* as a woman, for surely it is from here that the application to gay men emerged. This would follow a timeworn pattern in English, in which terms for women are refitted to indicate male weakness, male homosexuality, or both, almost as if it were foreordained. *Nellie* feeds the expression *nervous Nellie*, which referred to men; similarly a *weak sister* was a man, not a woman (and *sissy* is thus explained). *Nancy* and even *queen* also drifted into meaning "homosexual." *Pussy* sampled both interpretations, starting as "sweetie pie" and becoming a word for gay men for a while—recall Henry James referred to as a "pussy" for presumed homosexual relationships—before settling into meaning "coward." With women referred to as faggots, it was only a matter of time before, at least somewhere, the term came to be used, too, for men viewed as "feminine." Somewhere was the United States.

The first attestations are around the turn of the twentieth century. John Reed, American Communist writer, gives us our first example from 1913, as in: "Mr. Max Hoffmann is very anxious to put on their vaudeville revue, to do this it will be necessary to cut out the 'Garden of Girls' scene," he advised, but then shocks a bit today in adding on "also to eliminate 'The Fagot Number.'" Watching *Reds* (1981) you don't quite imagine Warren Beatty, portraying Reed, popping off with the word in that way (despite his tenaciously 1970s coiffure contrasting with the otherwise obsessive attention to period detail). Yet Reed's original letter shows (and not just once) that *faggot* was used as freely at the time as *nigger*.

Though Reed's usages are the earliest listed in the *Oxford English Dictionary*, we can assume that the practice did not emerge in 1913. We know that *faggot* in reference to gay men had been entrenched likely decades before, in the second half of the 1800s. Absent in the lexicographical annals is a recollection by a cop writing of his experiences as a bartender in the 1890s across from a gay bar of the period, Paresis Hall, near Cooper Square in New York City. When his coworker bartender refused two men their order of milk punches with eggs (what in the world was that?) and asked them to leave, one before departure "turned and said acidly, 'We may be fags but we're no common bartenders anyway.'"

The policeman recounting this in the 1930s also *refers* to gay men generically as "fags," and memory is slippery. The men in the 1890s may have used some other term, but if they did not, then this dates *faggot* about a generation before Reed's writing, and the men's offhand deployment of the term, including shortening it to *fag*, suggests that it was already well-worn, widely understood, and thus shortened, even then. This suggests that it emerged and settled in as early as the 1870s or before. It's just that no one would have had occasion to write it down—it belonged to the evanescence of oral culture.

Faggot gets from women to gay men, then, via a pathway of association still vivid today, where gayness is equated with weakness. In the late twentieth century people started saying "That's so gay" as an equivalent to "That's so lame," to the point that gay people began objecting to the phrase on principle, with a certain success—the expression is used less freely now than it was a generation ago.

Garden Paths

So—in the history of English, it is often charted as one of the oddest pathways of development from A to B that the word *silly* began as meaning "blessed," or that *nice* began as "idiotic" and *pretty* began as "cunning." But *faggot* surely takes the cake in beginning as a bundle of sticks and ending as a reference to gay men. No matter how dutifully one reads the evidence, it seems just a touch implausible.

We get a sense of how one might start calling people "faggots" when we imagine how easy it is today to refer to people as *piles of shit*, or more neutrally, *dirtbags*. When we putter around the garden, courtesy of Scotts and Miracle-Gro, we all know people whose essence could be summed up by those elastic sacks of soil. "You dirtbag!" we say. A thousand years ago the same sentiment yielded, based on what people then knew in their daily grind, "You faggot!"

Yet because the centrality of the woodpile to daily life long ago can be so hard to connect with, there are other explanations that get about, with shades of the shit boat. Gay men did not start being called faggots because they were once commonly burned at the stake amid burning bundles of sticks. For one, with apologies for the graphic nature of the information, in Merrie Olde England the more common penalty for homosexuality was hanging, not being burned alive.

But more to the point, the slur against gay men emerged not in medieval *Black Adder* England but in modern America. Who during the Gilded Age somewhere in New York or Boston or Chicago started calling gay men "faggots" based on vague notions *not actually in* books that gay men were roasted alive several centuries before on a different continent? To settle in, a new word or expression has to make immediate sense to listeners. Even if some tipsy, antiquarian soul tried to stir things up on a slow night by titling gay men after bundles of sticks alight—*Why, I imagine the medievals burning you amid faggots such that you came to resemble them; I deem you faggots!*—why would anyone else pick up on it? It'd have gone the way of *Mean Girls'* "fetch."

Too, it is unlikely that the British term *fag*, referring to a junior schoolboy slavishly serving a senior, contributed to the birth of America's slur. Again, the term for gay men arose in America, not England, and how richly would Britain's elite scholastic traditions have influenced the speech of ordinary American people, living across a vast ocean, and long before modern communications technology? If *fag* had come to America from Britain, then we would likely also chat about our week-*ends* and say things like "I shouldn't think so."

An idea that Yiddish's *faygele*, originally "little bird" and extended to gay men, at least helped nudge *faggot* into a gay meaning has the same problem. Jewish people were a perse-cuted and despised (mostly) immigrant minority in America in 1900. Beyond the terms they offered for things that had no En-glish name, such as ones for foods (*bagel*) or personality types (*schlemiel*), why would Americans take up their words as re-placements for ones they already had? *Faygele* to any non-Jewish person at the turn of the twentieth century would have been as exotic and unnecessary as the Black American usage of *cock* to refer to women's as well as men's parts. There were plenty of nasty words for gay men before *faggot*, which included *degenerate*, *sodomite*, *nancy*, and even *homosexualist*, intrigu-ing in implying some kind of occult occupation.

As one hates to throw cold water, it bears mentioning that slurs against gay men can have some of the most unexpected etymologies of any words in this book, even if Yiddish is unlikely to have provided one. The British *bugger* traces not to mosquitoes and beetles but to, of all things, "Bulgarian," with the idea that Eastern Orthodox people were sexually depraved in some way. And *ponce* likely started as the French *pensionnaire* (pronounced "pahn-syo-nair"), when in the nineteenth century it had the specific connotation of a man who lived off of women's earnings. This originally referred to a pimp, but the situation was considered a subservient and thus "weak" one, and so, you know.

On *Cocksucker*

The reader will note that I neglect none other than one of George Carlin's classic seven curse words, *cocksucker*. Certainly this qualifies as a quintessential slur against gay men, such that one processes it as Carlin's name-check of anti-gay language and almost wonders why *faggot* didn't make the list.

But then *nigger* didn't, either, and it's because Carlin was working before slurs had become profane as opposed to just inappropriate. And in broader view, what *cocksucker* meant to him was only diagonally connected to homosexuality. Here is a term that has reversed the trajectory of most ugly terms in its orbit. Generally, a word connoting weakness—such as, unfortunately, those related to being a woman—comes to refer to being gay, as in *pussy* and *faggot* itself. But *cocksucker* originated as referring to homosexuality, and then seems to have almost immediately been extended to general weakness.

The action in question is too specific and loaded to gracefully extend to what one would lob at a woman in anger. "Whore" is one thing, but a charge of sin entails personal enjoyment, and while the "whore" is supposedly evil in liking intercourse, the female "cocksucker" would presumably be only affording the man such enjoyment. Say that her affording that privilege to any Tom, *Dick*, and Harry could qualify as the source of an insult, and yet a certain cognitive dissonance remains between the woman as vulgar on the one hand and a "good time" on the other. That dissonance has, in English at least, prevented *cocksucker* from becoming a slur against women.

Hence the *cocksucker* is a man. As with *faggot*, its origin story is American. The *Oxford English Dictionary*'s first instance is from a gay diarist in Massachusetts in 1885 recounting a man who "told me in so many words that he is 'C—sucker' & that he loves and enjoys that d—d custom so revolting to every right minded person." But around the same time, court documents in New York state record a man saying "You dirty Irish cocksucker, if you don't have less to say, I'll fix you."

From then on, there are both gay cocksuckers and people called cocksuckers simply as a general insult, as generic as roughly *you fuck*, or even an early equivalent of *asshole*. A detective reported a night in 1911 when at a saloon in New York City there was a man who:

> *had his right hand on the left breast of a women [sic] who wore a low-cut evening dress. The breasts were exposed so you could see the shape of the woman's two breasts; you couldn't see the nipple of her breast, and he had his hand over there and she said "Get away from here, you cocksucker. What do you think this is, free lunch?"*

Clearly she wasn't calling this man a homosexual—*cocksucker* had quickly come to just mean someone who was generally annoying, wrong. This is the meaning Carlin knew, and as utterly modern as he was in his day, his inclusion of the word now qualifies as antique. Writing two decades into the twenty-first century as a middle-aged person, I can confidently say that in my verbal existence, neither as a slur for gay men nor as an equivalent of *asshole* has *cocksucker* been a living word. It has joined *pillecock* and *bulldyke* (see page 227) as the slang of yesteryear, helping furnish the slip between Carlin's seven bad words and this book's nine.

So why isn't it "dicksucker," given that, as we have seen, *cock* is now a tad archaic except as a pornographic term? It's for the same reason that we refer to *mother wit* as meaning common sense, not humor. *Wit* first meant knowledge, and while the word alone morphed into referring to the amusing, in expressions it remained frozen, as in, also, to keep one's wits about one.

Cocksucker was minted in the nineteenth century before *dick* was au courant, and so quickly stopped referring to actual cocks that there was no impulse to keep its penile reference current. *Cocktease* and *cock ring* are analogous—both terms would have *dick* if coined today.

Dyke: The Most Successful Appropriation

The reader may also notice that I have not included the female equivalent of *faggot*—*dyke*—as one of our Big Nine Nasties. This is because *dyke*, for all of its injuriousness, does not quite qualify as profane. We do not process it as shudderingly unutterable. It is not out-and-out taboo.

While we can list a number of mean words for gay men, there are many fewer for gay women. There seems to be less motivation to create them, out of a sense that lesbianism is perhaps less threatening than male homosexuality. Male homosexuality is associated with weakness, with men supposedly taking on the mannerisms and sexual role of what is tragically so often considered the weaker sex. Lesbianism, then, perhaps rankles less in that women are already seen as being in the down position.

In regards to put-downs becoming terms of affection, *dyke* differs from *nigger* and *faggot* (and *bitch*) in being an especially successful appropriation. Black men may refer to Black people as "niggers" in a layered way, with contempt, even if amused and tolerant, as close to the surface as affection. Meanwhile, whole books, eternal media conversations, and episodic dust-ups pivot on the word's eternal usage as a slur.

Gay men referring to one another as "faggots," "fags," and "homos" is similarly multifaceted. Gay activist Larry Kramer titled a 1978 book *Faggots*, and I once heard a gay man say that his party was "Just a bunch of fags having a good time." In the 1990s, there arose in San Francisco a theater troupe calling themselves the Pomo Afro Homos, as in postmodern African American homosexuals. Allies of gay men venture similar usages, with affection. The now aging term *fag hag* for a woman with many gay male friends was a perfect example, especially in that it was often used as a self-description, in which contempt rather than love for gay men would have been unlikely. Wondering if I should share this, I will recount that when I was in college, I was dancing at a party with a female pal who had a lot of gay friends. I said I was going to go to the bathroom, and she retorted, "You better come back or I'm gonna send a homo in there to fuck you up the butt!" She in no sense meant it literally; it was said with affection both for me and for gay men, and I doubt any gay man listening (at least to the whole exchange, who knew both of us) would have taken offense.

But: for many gay men, just behind the affection in these appropriations lurks the self-hatred of *The Boys in the Band*. A robust literature expresses discomfort with such "affectionate" usage, with many gay men having the same hard time separating the term of endearment from memories of being subject to the slur as many Black people have regarding the N-word. We need only think of what my friend said to me that night in 1984. With all due acknowledgment of my friend's innocent intent, was it quite gay-*supportive* to posit a gay man forcing himself upon someone in a bathroom?

Plus the slur connotation of *faggot* lives on, as does the sense that to be a gay man is a social sin. Young straight men still append "No homo" to social media messages praising one another. The straight-guy "I love ya, man!" is more heart-on-the-sleeve than the pipe-smoking 1950s man would have known, but the sentiment still comes with an assurance that one is not venturing into something so apparently unacceptable as homosexuality.

Here is where the uniqueness of *dyke* comes in. Many lesbians refer to one another as *dykes* with an unalloyed pride and comfort. The term comes with a genuine sense of smile and acceptance, transformed from its emergence as a term of abuse, used in jokes, documented as a true transformation of the earlier variety. That lesbianism is perceived as *somewhat* less hair-raising a transgression than being male and gay certainly has helped *dyke* acquire this truly appropriated status.

In a parallel to the episode when a Black man working in the Milwaukee public school system was fired for "using" *nigger*, in 2004, the United States Patent and Trademark Office tried to deny the organization Dykes on Bikes the trademark for the name, out of a sense that *dyke* qualified as a slur. The organization dredged up miles of documentation confirming that the word no longer always qualifies as what I would call profane and won their case in 2005. These days, lesbians proudly wear the word emblazoned on T-shirts—less imaginable of *nigger* or *faggot* except in aggressive irony. A book called *Nigger* is hot peppers, as would be a book published today—as opposed to during the Carter administration—called *Faggot*.* A book called *Dyke*, though, could be written with satisfaction by someone like lesbian writer and artist Alison Bechdel, who in fact penned a long-running comic called *Dykes to Watch Out For*.

Queer, too, has gone from insult even past term of affection, to a neutral descriptor one might use in a legal brief, where *dyke* would be less appropriate despite its reformation. In the acronym LGBTQ, *queer* takes its place alongside *lesbian*, *gay*, *bisexual*, and *transgender* as a word anyone can be comfortable uttering. However, the transformation of *dyke* is more revolutionary. The mainstreaming of *queer*—"We're here, we're queer, get used to it"—has been gender-neutral, discretely eliding the stark and complex differences between the experiences of gay women as opposed to gay men. English needed a word like

---

*Note also that Larry Kramer's book title *Faggots* would be considered less marketable today than in 1978, another indication that the word, however used, has gone from naughty to outright taboo.

queer, but issues of identity will always have gender as a fulcrum. *Dyke* on a T-shirt asserts a victory over matters of both same-sex preference and being a woman. The appropriation responds to a discrimination that cuts more deeply for a gay woman than that against gay people in general.

From Dagger to Dyke?

Yet as always, *dyke* as slur remains in power, and thus requires a look. As it happens, unlike with the front-window curse words, the etymology of *dyke* is not merely obscure, but unknowable. We are mired in guesswork.

It first appears in print in 1906, already in full flower as a dismissive slur against lesbians. That year, a book on "human sexuality" informed readers that "in American homosexual argot, female inverts, or lesbian lovers, are known euphemistically as 'bulldykers,' whatever that may mean: at least that is their sobriquet in the 'Red Light' district of Philadelphia."

After this come attestations from Harlem. Carl Van Vechten's notorious *Nigger Heaven* of 1926 refers to the "bulldiker," and two years later, Claude McKay's *Home to Harlem* has a character saying that two things he doesn't understand are "a bulldyking woman and a faggoty man." In 1935, our blues pal Lucille Bogan enters the scene once again, eluding our official lexicographers, with her song "B.D. Woman's Blues," celebrating what that abbreviation stood for—bulldyke—as "They got a

head like a sweet angel and they walk just like a natural man."
(Bogan, almost seeming as if she wanted to cover as many of the
terms in this book as she could, elsewhere in her oeuvre name-
checked *ass* and *dick* as well.)

But before these examples, silence. We don't know whether
Andrew Jackson randily referred to "bulldykes" or "dykes" when
joking with pals, or what word he would have used instead. As
such, attempts to make sense of why *dyke* is used to refer to gay
women have been somewhat athletic, and frankly almost funny
in the grand scheme of things. One's job is to also account for
the competing forms from the old days, such as *bulldiker, bulldyke* (which I grew up hearing from older Black people in Philadelphia), and *bulldagger.*

One proposal is that the reference is to the dike that the boy
stuck his finger into in the Hans Brinker story because, well...
let's just allow us our own mental pictures and move on. Then
there is an idea that the dagger in *bulldagger* was a metaphorical reference to a woman's having a penis on some level—or
even, regarding the occasional variant *bulldicker*, to women
whose relevant anatomy is (presumably) of such a size that they
can use it as a phallus.

Could *bulldyke* have been a corruption of the name of the
Celtic warrior queen Boadicea? Or, perhaps *dike* emerged as a
slangy pronunciation of *hermaphrodite*. I kid you not—the sug-
gestion is that *hermaphrodite* was at some point mispronounced
as *morphodite*, which was further mangled into *morphodike*,
and you can take it from there. Or—was it that the *bull* was the

one that refers to fakery, and that *bulldagger* meant a fake dagger as in a fake penis?

We will never know for sure but all of that sounds kind of silly, and my sense of how words acquire and transform their meanings teaches that we seek the most plausible series of steps, each one as mundane as possible, such that none require Gaslight Era barflies comparing people to obscure figures from British history like Boadicea (*Say, honey, did anybody ever tell you you look like Anne of Cleves?*).

By the 1890s, and likely long before, *dike* was a slang term for the vulva for obvious reasons. It would have been plausible for lesbians to thus be referred to as "dikers"—one day, this *Archaeopteryx* form just might be unearthed in print. Equally plausible would have been for this, after it got a little old, to be reinforced with *bull*, in reference to masculine demeanor. This would especially have been the case in that the term was originally applied mainly to lesbians of male-like appearance or manner. That the term *bull bitch* got around for a while in the early twentieth century makes this reconstruction even more likely. It may also have been that *bulldiker* was built directly upon *dike* for vulva, without an intermediate *diker* stage. Etymology must allow for such possibilities, don't you know.

Whichever it was, after *dike* for vulva went out of circulation, which appears to have been as quickly as *wang* for the penis did a hundred years later, to new generations, *bulldiker* would have ceased to make immediate sense, in the same way that with *threshold* we neither know what was being threshed, what it held, or the fact that the word did not actually even start as a combination of *thresh* and *hold* at all. In cases like that, conditions are ripe for driftings and misinterpretations. If dikes were no longer vulvas, then the *-diker* part of *bulldiker* would have easily been shorn a bit, much of the time, as just *-dike*, and hence *bulldike*. This would have been in line with the tendency we saw in regard to *fuck* and other swears to be single-syllable words flanked by hard consonants. All knew what *bull* means; the *-dike* part would have sounded like a more robust contribution to the nastiness, especially in taking on what the Anglophone subconsciously feels as a bad word's proper shape.

If a "butch" lesbian was associated with a certain aggressive-ness, then especially when the term was also used most in after-hours, underworld realms, *bulldiker* could easily have been recast as *bulldagger* out of the same visceral desire to make sense of a strange word that led some to call asparagus "sparrow grass." One might drift into saying "bull*dagger*" out of (1) not knowing what a *diker* was and (2) a sense of the dagger as threatening—the "butch" lesbian as a weapon. One indication that *bulldagger* was a reinterpretation is that it appears in print only in the 1930s, decades after *bulldike*.

Almost inevitably, if *hamburger* became *burger*, *pillecock* became *cock*, and the association of lesbians with bulls was al-ways a tad strained, then soon *bulldike* would become just *dike*, and later settle upon the *dyke* spelling. This would render the word a perfect example of the quintessential sound of an En-glish curse word—short with a crisp start and finish.

Language Change for Real

Returning to the original word of focus in this chapter, our closing lesson is how it has traveled a fascinating pathway from object to slur to term of affection. Plus that is only in America, as opposed to an alternate pathway in Great Britain leading to meatballs and cigarettes!

Their *fag* for cigarette, for example, is from the term *fag-end* referring to the frayed end of a rope or a stray piece of hanging cloth. The cigarette *fag* referred to what Americans call butts, a used and thus "frayed" cigarette. The origin of the *fag* in *fag-end* is unknown. Words that are both Anglo-ancient and short have a way of resisting the etymologist—believe it or not, we will likely never know just where simple words like *dog* and *bad* came from, either.

However, I hereby venture that the source of *fag-end* was the same old bundle of sticks, and that what has discouraged that hypothesis is a certain oddness or marginality the modern person cannot help perceiving in those bundles. Given how central they were to medieval existence, and how foreign the idea was that the word would ever be applied to homosexuality, it is hardly implausible that the frayed end of a rope looked to them like a miniature version of, well, a faggot. These are the same people who processed dummy soldiers as akin to bundles of sticks, and if anything, seems *more* intuitive.

As such, a chart of how that original word has evolved would look like this:

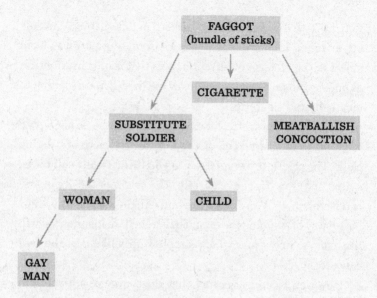

Where a word for a bunch of kindling now refers, all at once, to cigarettes, meatballs, and gay men.

Profanity, as always, is ripe—and the last of our Big Nine words is no exception.

* 8 *

BEING IN TOTAL CONTROL,
HONEY!

I t'd be great if that's where the word came from, as the website Heartless Bitches International teaches us with tongue in cheek. We all know the truth is more mundane. Our final profanity is one more word grievously applied to women, and it no more began as a confident acronym than did *shit*, *fuck*, or *nigger* ("never ignorant getting goals accomplished," as Tupac Shakur and Jadakiss proposed). Rather, it started with dogs.

Beyond that, the etymologist knows a brick wall is likely. It seems like it has three consonants at the end of it, *bitch* does. The *t*, *c*, and *h*. But that's just the tragedy of English spelling—*tch* is just one sound. And that means that *bitch* is one of those words—as in, one vowel sandwiched between two tart consonant sounds, *b* and *ch*.

That kind of word has a way of eluding the historian. Words are like cars after pile-up crashes, smashed from both ends. So often they started as two or even more words, with heavy usage amid rapid speech over long periods of time scrunching them up into single ones. "Bye," we say, when that started as *God be with you*, which contracted to *goodbye* and then just *bye*. *Darn* started as *eternal damnation*. *Daisy* started as *day's eye*. Sometimes it's just that a short word started as a longer one: Latin's *domina*—"female master of the house"—became English's *dame*.

But we would never know any of that if we couldn't see it happening in written records of ancient languages like Latin and Old English. If we need to know what happened even earlier, given that the further back we go the slimmer the corpora of written languages tend to be, we often end up nowhere.

That's the case with *bitch*, where we know that the source is Old English's *bicge*, meaning, as we all know as the "core" meaning of the word, female dog. In Old English, the *cg* meant *ch*, and back that far we get one extra sound, the "uh" at the end, represented by the *-e*. So the car wasn't quite as crushed yet, but before that we know nothing. There is no indication in the languages that birthed Old English of a word like that, no evidence of a grandfather word from Ukraine that spread not only to England but throughout Europe.

There is instead a word like it in one of the passel of kittens that Old English had evolved *alongside*, as one of the Germanic languages. That was Old Norse, father of what now is Swedish, Norwegian, and Danish as well as Icelandic. Some scholars venture that Old English got the word from their rendition, but there is no mic-drop reason to suppose that early Brits needed a word from Viking invaders for female doggies. Just as likely, they had always had their *bicges* from some earlier iteration we will never know.

What we do know is that what subsequently happened to the Old English word for female dog neatly illustrates much that we have seen in this book, serving as a kind of final-exam object lesson in how profanity works in English. The range of usages of *bitch* today is wider than we often have reason to consider, and all that range is predictable given the principles of profanity, as it were, that we have seen. We must imagine a medieval person in the peculiar position of being familiar with the principles of lexical change in this book, who would be in a position to anticipate pretty much everything that has happened to the word in the past thousand years. To wit, of *bicge*, our canny Æthelstan could breezily predict, or at least not find at all surprising, that...

It Will Become a Term of Contempt for Women.

It is generally known that *bitch* "technically" means female dog, but it is never used that way in polite company in America (it is somewhat more allowed among veterinary professionals in the United Kingdom). It is one more thing that can make Middle and Early Modern English peculiar reading, in that *bitch* is used as freely as *mare* today. In 1397, in a proto-encyclopedia of sorts, we learn of the unfortunate situation of puppies born blind—"The bytche bringeth forth blynde whelpes." In 1575 we were taught (spelling modernized): "If you would have fair hounds, you must first have a fair Bitch, which is of a good kind, strong and well proportioned in all parts, having her ribs and her flanks great and large."

The first attestation of the word applied to women comes down to us from about 1400, in a put-down from one woman to another in a play: "Whom calleste thou queine, skabde biche?" ("Who are you calling queen, miserable bitch?") In 1675, Thomas Hobbes, someone we might not associate with the lively or the demotic (no one would take *Leviathan* to the beach) translated Ulysses in *The Odyssey* sneering to Penelope, "You bitch."

It is sometimes claimed that at first, *bitch* as applied to women referred to female dogs in heat. There is no evidence that the comparison was that specific. However, the original metaphor does seem to have been based on a female dog's multiple partners, given a certain tendency in earlier examples. A book of religious instruction from 1650 teaches that "a whore is compared to a bitch, that hath many following her," while back in 1581 one read of Roman empress Messaline who (spelling modernized):

> *found by proof that her husband was insufficient and unable to satisfy her lecherous desires, by my counsel often-times she disguised herself into men's apparel, and went to*

the common stewes [brothels], whereas she abused her body
with a great number, returning back no better than a bitch,
and vaunted that she had vanquished and gone beyond all
the whores in the house of bawdery.

This sheds light on what kind of hunger and needs was meant in, for example, a woman growling in a play of 1575, "The pox light on her whore's sides, a pestilence and mischief! / Come out, thou hungry, needy bitch!"

Thus *bitch* joined the legions of words in English referring to women that have drifted into contempt. Not all of them become profane; the tendency is even broader. *Housewife*, uttered an awful lot over a great deal of time and seasoned by unsavory assumptions, became *hussy*. A *mistress* was once what it looks like, a female master; now it is something else and ickier. A *tart* started as a jam-tart, meaning "good-looking woman." But after a while, it got both shorter and nastier and wound up out on the pavement. *Queen* was a rare exception here, beginning as simply "woman." However, it was an exception that proves the rule.

Bitch as a slur, once settled in, has been especially widely discussed in regard to its use by rappers, where it has often been used as practically a synonym for *woman*. "Life ain't nothin' but bitches and money," N.W.A's famous lyric from "Gangsta Gangsta" went. Just as famously, rappers performatively distorted the word into "bee-yotch," an outcome that the word would never have reached via how sounds in words normally change.

It was as if they were not only saying but playing, to demonstrate their sense of impunity.

This treatment of *bitch*, though, hardly emerged with rap in the 1970s. It was a direct descendant of the exact same usage of the word underground in Black "toasts," which were street-corner slam poetry once as lustily embraced by Black men as rap is now. A young Black guy today happily chants the latest raps; his grandfather may well have been just as eagerly chanting toasts. And these could be as nasty as some raps have been, including in their reveling in and abusing the word *bitch*. A famous one had it that "Say, you got to rule that bitch, you got to school that bitch, you got to teach her the Golden Rule, you got to stomp that bitch, you got to tromp that bitch, and use her like you would a tool."

Of course most toasts weren't that vicious, but as a genre, *bitch* occupied the same place in them as in raps like those of N.W.A Black scholar of the toast Roger Abrahams indicatively glossaried *bitch* as "any woman. As used here without usual pejorative connotations." Most today would find it hard to miss at least a degree of the "pejorative" in pretty much all references to "bitches" in toasts, but Abrahams was getting at the simple fact that the word was used freely in reference to all women, or at least ones regarded as sexual beings. It depicted women kept "in their place," directly equivalent to the way white men at the time were using "cunts"—recall the 1911 police report about "cunts" crowding a dance floor and Henry Roth on a "pretty cunt" walking up the street. Sub in *bitch* for *cunt*, and the old days become these days. Perhaps call it evidence of the races coming together, in that now the same white men, raised on hip-hop, are more likely to use *bitch* in this function.

But even then, toasts were never the only place that *bitch* was used as a dismissive term for a female person in Black culture. Black women were using it that way as well. Example: queen of Black blues singers Bessie Smith is recorded as having said in a fight with a female lover: "The hell with you, bitch. I got twelve women on this show and I can have one every night if I want it." I think also of a tweet *by a woman* that got around in 2020, reading "bitches be like 'bitches be like' and then be the bitches that be like."*

It Will Go Abstract and Connote General Worthlessness or Nuisance.

We tend to use *shit* in the abstract. The flow of modern English would lead a Martian to think *shit* referred simply to worthless or annoying things and ideas, and that the association with feces was a later development via comparison. It'd be a natural conclusion given how much more frequently we say things like

---

*Imagine trying to explain what that sentence means to Theodore—or Eleanor—Roosevelt. And endless thanks to my *Lexicon Valley* listener Calleigh Mentzer-Tootle for the heads-up.

I'm sick of that shit and *he's always bringing up his shit*, whereas how often, really, do we discuss excrement? And when we do, we usually say *poop*.

Bitch has had an analogous development, in that from referring to a woman giving offense, it has come, for one, to refer to *things* giving offense, usually resisting control. *It's a bitch to steer that thing. Life's a bitch, and then you die. That bitch is really stuck in there.* (This last in reference to a large rock in the ground.) And just as sexism goes way back, so does this usage. In 1962, it was entrenched enough that "This afternoon's been a bitch" got by the censors in the film *Hud* when the word in its literal meaning would have been less likely to,* and ultimately we must leash it to no less than figures like Byron, Kipling, and Beckett.

Yes, them. Lord Byron referred in an 1814 letter to his luck as linked to "my bitch of a star." In 1904, Rudyard Kipling, cherished by generations for his stalwart language, wrote in a now obscure story, "After eight years, my father, cheated by your bitch of a country, he found out who was the upper dog in South

---

*Less likely because the dam was already crumbling by this time: *Hush… Hush, Sweet Charlotte* of the same period (1964) had Bette Davis memorably calling Olivia de Havilland a "vile, sorry little bitch." Indicatively, in the 2010s, the real de Havilland sued upon being depicted in the television miniseries *Feud* as referring to her sister Joan Fontaine as a bitch. Her doing so would have been around when things had opened up enough that Davis was hauling it off in *Hush… Hush*. Yet to de Havilland, coming of age in the 1920s and 1930s, to be publicly depicted using such language at any time in her life felt like slander.

Africa." Samuel Beckett's *Waiting for Godot* included the line, "That's how it is on this bitch of an earth."

The abstraction goes further in a change in part of speech, to the verb "to bitch." This has come in many flavors. It would seem that every shade of meaning comprised in the noun *bitch* has contributed to metaphorical developments of a verbal nature: inferiority, obstacle, nuisance, complaint, and sexual inappropriateness.

As early as Middle English, Chaucer referred to cursed dice as "bitched bones two," while in 1500 one of the Townley plays is even more specific, with "I was falsly begylyd with thise byched bones / Ther cursyd thay be." The idea was that to be cursed was to be consigned to the inferior level of woman.

Related to this was *bitch* meaning to ruin or spoil, more common in Britain than in America. In 1823, a guide to British slang instructs "to bitch a business, to spoil it, by aukwardness, fear, or want of strength," and as late as 1964, Dennis Wheatley has a character in his *They Used Dark Forces* grumble, "To bitch Hitler's last chance of winning the war I'd willingly spend a year down a coal mine on bread and water." A variation has also been to give someone a hard time, especially verbally. In Evelyn Waugh's *A Handful of Dust* from 1934, Brenda is proud of how she handles a gentleman who is a challenge, breezily noting that she is in fact "bitching" him. Graham Greene's Helen in *The Heart of the Matter* says, "I thought you were never coming. I bitched you so."

That usage has not been alien to American English. The

underread Dawn Powell had "She's been bitched by everyone else" in her *Turn, Magic Wheel*, although that was in 1936 and the line reads as antique today. Interestingly, however, Americans (like Brits) are familiar with the concept of *botching something*, and with *bitch* signifying "to ruin," a relationship with *botch* seems hardly impossible, even if undocumented and thus uncertain.

More common in America has been a different offshoot: *bitch* meaning "to complain," which appears to be a twentieth-century development. As to the sexual descendant, we would assume that in modern English the verb of choice would be to *whore*. But there is a chance element in these things, and it would be almost surprising if Anglophone men at some point had not spoken of going out a-bitching. And, in fact, they did—in a poem of 1675, Charles Cotton had Prometheus cawing to Jupiter, "Why, then, to cure thy Itching / Jove, thou now art going a Bitching."

Thus *life's a bitch* and *Will you quit bitching?* are but hors d'oeuvres to the proliferation of this word.

It Will Be Classified as a "Bad Word."

Technically, *bitch* contradicts one of our dictums. Profanity starts as being about religion and later the body, but *bitch* refers to neither of those. Then, slurs become a new form of profanity—but *bitch* in reference to women was considered unfit for polite company long before our other slurs became taboo.

This is because it gets in through the back door as being about the body. With its source in reference to the reproductive habits of dogs, plus an implied sense of untowardness about a woman's sexuality—this being the source of so much animadversion toward women—the word has always felt somewhat carnal. This is despite its literal meaning, and despite that after the Middle Ages it has been used as often as not to refer to a woman as being irritating rather than "wanton." Its redolence is that no matter a woman's status or attainments, she is "just" something, and where what men call women is concerned, that "just" refers to one thing—the same one that once created the terms *white* and *dark meat* (to avoid referring to breasts, thighs, and limbs).

American popular culture between the wars nicely indicates the niche the word occupied before the late 1960s. It's hard to choose a single best line from the film *The Women* of 1939, but most if forced to would likely go for one when formerly kept woman Crystal Allen has final words with Park Avenue matrons: "There's a name for you ladies, but it isn't used in high society—outside of a kennel." It was a priceless way of saying what could not be said in a movie.*

---

*It even leads one to think for at least a millisecond or two about the development from *bitch* to rappers' "*bee*-yotch."

Things were a little randier on the stage, out of reach of the Code that muzzled the cinema. I must cite one more time the deservedly unknown musical hit *Follow the Girls* of 1944, in which a tenor states of one character "She is a witch," after which a ballet dancer cracks, "You mean bitch!" But that was meant for a laugh, in a show pitched to horny soldiers on leave out for some fun.*

A further summation of the peekaboo nature of how the word was processed at this time is the 1932 Cole Porter stage musical that inspired the Astaire-Rogers film *The Gay Divorcee*, called just *Gay Divorce*. In one song, a wry lady sings of a certain Mr. and Mrs. Fitch that "Now men who once knew Missus Fitch / Refer to her as a bitch. / While the girls who once loved Mister Fitch / Say he always was a son of a bitch." Porter, a man of the Café Society theater scene, intended the lady just selling the word *bitch* across the footlights. However, in rehearsals, the singer** arranged for the drummer to hit a good smack on both

---

*If that character could say that onstage in 1944, then some will wonder whether in the stage version of *The Women*, which premiered in 1936 a few years before the film, Crystal just hauled off with the word. Alas, no. She just said, "You're just a cat, like all the rest of us!" And no, Crystal was not played in the stage version by anyone as fierce and interesting to us now as Joan Crawford—rather, it was some Betty Lawford (neat that her last name rhymed with Joan's), replaced as the show played on by the equally forgotten Claire Carleton. If you crave something memorable anyway, in the original production you could have caught a teenaged Jacqueline Susann in a bit part.

**It was Luella Gear, whom fans of the Fred and Ginger films will recognize as the sarcastic lady of a certain age in one of the lesser entries in the series, *Carefree* (1938).

instances, making it unhearable. The original score parts the orchestra members played from in 1932 still exists, and those beats are indeed penciled over the drummer's part—you can almost hear the cast tittering at their joke. So coy—one part Broadway and one part Hollywood. And one part the rest of America, in that the sheet music for living room pianists had "witch" and "son of the rich." No *bitch* in print, outside of a kennel.

It Will Switch Genders.

We have seen how *pussy* and *cunt* have been applied to men to connote inferiority, out of a medieval guideline that to be female is to be lesser than male and thus inherently lame. *Bitch* has been no exception.

The most "literal" extension in this vein is associated with prison, where the "bitch" is an inmate who engages in the submissive position during sex with other inmates. Here, the meaning components of subservience and sexual deviance combine. This qualifies mainly as a local kind of slang, even though it can encompass the idea that a man is another one's "bitch" amid other endeavors.

Today, to more people it brings a less specific and less acridly hostile connotation, where one man joshingly refers to some others as "bitches" as a kind of preening maintenance of pecking order. Someone I know summarized one of the volumes in Robert Caro's magisterial Lyndon Johnson biography, *Master of the Senate*, with a kind of conversational GIF in which Johnson strode into the Senate chamber hollering, "I'm Lyndon Johnson, bitcheeezzzz . . . !" One senses this never actually happened, but it nicely encapsulated this modern usage, à la throwing down a full house, or a man showing a photo on his phone of an especially attractive woman he is dating, and yelling "How about *that*, bitches—whoo!"

That gender jump isn't as novel as it may seem. Men were referring to other ones as "bitches" as far back as the Renaissance if not before, although without the patina of vernacular affection implied these days. Around 1500 a man is recorded as growling, "He is a schrewed byche, In fayth, I trow, he be a wyche." (It is no accident that over time, *shrewd* came to be a compliment while *shrewish*, from the same word but mainly applied to women, became a slam.) Robert Louis Stevenson in *Catriona* had David called "a queer bitch after a' [all], and I have no mind of meeting with the like of ye." In James Joyce's *A Portrait of the Artist as a Young Man*, Stephen's father asks Stephen's sister, "Is your lazy bitch of a brother gone out yet?" (Stephen replies, "He has a curious idea of genders if he thinks bitch is masculine.")

We must not neglect *son of a bitch*, which is pretty close to just *bitch*. The literal meaning is so dimly considered that the *bitch* part is all that stands out. Nowhere is this clearer than in the southern US rendition "sum-bitch," where all notions of the filial are muddied over. It seems to get around that Jackie Gleason was the originator of this pronunciation with his Buford T.

Justice character in the *Smokey and the Bandit* movies, but this falls apart in that you can also hear it in Strother Martin's famous line in *Cool Hand Luke* (1967): "I can be a good guy, or I can be one real mean sum-bitch." It is a Southern pronunciation that likely traces quite a ways back.

The historical attestations of the original term *son of a bitch* seem almost designed to display a gradual process in which a full expression coalesces into essentially a single word. It begins with citations such as one from the Bard himself, in *King Lear*, where Kent calls Oswald "nothing but the composition of a knaue, begger, coward, pander, and the sonne and heire of a mungrell bitch." Meanwhile in a Beaumont and Fletcher play, Uberto must specify of two other men that "They had no mothers, they are the sons of bitches."

These earliest references sound like Mr. Burns savoring his first taste of "iced cream" or Chauncey Gardner reading the Black boys' belligerent note in *Being There*. But it settled in fast. A novel of 1834, *Peter Simple*, has "You burgoo-eating, pea-soup-swilling, trouser-scrubbing son of a bitch." Well, hello! Then fast-forward: if you were assigned *The Grapes of Wrath* in school, you read, "They's a big son-of-a-bitch of a peach orchard I worked in." Vast trees to pick from as, well, bitches. How *dare* they!

Meanwhile, the trash-talk usage of *bitch* has already softened in some circles into a friendly greeting of exactly the sort that *son of a bitch* long ago evolved into. Just as George's friends on the *Seinfeld* episode greeted one another with "Hey, bastards," as I write a teen woman can greet an assemblage of male and female friends with "Hey, bitches!" (or at least I have seen this). Here the word has become both an equalizer and gender-neutral, ever more a mere shadow of something that began referring to an animal and afterward was a term of aggression and dismissal.

It Will Be Used as a Term of Affection.

"If he thinks he's gonna mess with us, he chose the wrong bitches," a friend of mine once said, who for the record is a proper sort who cherishes Trollope and Sondheim. DON'T JUST BE A BITCH—BE A CRITICAL BITCH, read the manifesto of a zine published at Stanford when I was a graduate student there. Then there was the brief fame of the health-oriented cookbook and blog authored by two women who called themselves "Skinny Bitch in the Kitch."

All of these represent *bitch* taking the same path as *nigger*, *faggot*, and *dyke*, transformed into a term of in-group affection. Not as successfully as *dyke*, in that *bitch* can still sting hard. However, its appropriation has been more deliberate, and given how sad the history of most attempts to change language have been, its success is impressive.

Jo Freeman, a feminist lawyer amidst the "Women's Lib" era in 1968, summarized the new attitude in a way that must be quoted in full:

A Bitch takes shit from no one. You may not like her, but you cannot ignore her.... [Bitches] have loud voices and often use them. Bitches are not pretty.... Bitches seek their identity strictly thru themselves and what they do. They are subjects, not objects ... Often they do dominate other people when roles are not available to them which more creatively sublimate their energies and utilize their capabilities. More often they are accused of domineering when doing what would be considered natural by a man.

There is no similarly explicit statement announcing the appropriation of *nigger, faggot,* or *dyke,* and this one, from what is titled "The BITCH Manifesto," represented a fresh notion of female "disruptiveness." It cast as antique every television show of the era that portrayed women who wanted something other than being submissive housewives as "crazy," "pushy," and unfeminine.

Life hardly transformed overnight: in the late 1970s, Hillary Rodham was reviled in Arkansas for not taking her husband's name. But thought was quietly, if slowly, changing, made clear from little things like the new term *bitchin'. Bitchin'* conveyed that complaining, being obstreperous, was to be encouraged, directly parallel to, and perhaps even inspired by, the inversion of *bad* to mean *good* in Black English, a bit of sixties-to-seventies slang publicized to a degree awkwardly dwarfing the brevity, typical of slang, of its reign.

Bitchin', too, was typically evanescent, shining in the 1970s and obsolete a generation later. But the comparison to the Black English *bad* is inexact, in that the California surfing culture that gave rise to *bitchin'* was that of the 1950s, when mainstream English was less influenced by Black speech than it is today, rather than the stoner Venice Beach seventies scene. The 1957 novel that the Gidget franchise was based on had: "It was a bitchen day too. The sun was out and all that." But still, the term only took off after Americans drank in at least a hint that *bitch* could be something to be proud of, even far away from beaches or Sally Field.

Subtler and yet just as "fierce," in the tradition of Jo Freeman, has been the concept of the "betch" in the 2010s, popularized by the Betches Love This website. The vowel change represents how the "bitches" in question pronounce the word, where the *ih* vowel has drifted quietly to *eh* among younger American women. You have to squint to catch this, but along with vocal fry it is key in indicating, instantly though subliminally, that a voice is younger. Think of a young American woman whose pronunciation of "just a bit" sounds more like, if not exactly like, "just a bet." Then that same woman's pronunciation of *eh* has shifted as well, to something more like the *a* in *cat*. "Let's go to bed" will sound more like "Let's go to bad."

As such, *bitch* becomes "betch," and the Betches Love This trope is that women who say it that way have certain qualities, and they reflect a proud conception of what a bitch is. Namely—"materialistic, sustains herself on iced coffee and Diet Coke, and believes the three cardinal rules in life are 'don't be easy,' 'don't be poor,' and 'don't be ugly.'" The "betch" under this definition, despite whatever triviality one notes, at least doesn't take any shit.*

We are told that the betch admires the Elle Woods character in the film *Legally Blonde*, smugly and cluelessly obsessed with appearance to the point of it constituting a kind of expertise, and smart enough that she gets over the hottie jerk who rejects her as not "serious" enough and instead chooses the brilliant but low-born fella who adores her.**

Relevant is also Black folk culture expert Roger Abrahams deigning much usage of *bitch* "neutral." In this, he was influenced by its appearance in Black blues songs—Lucille Bogan being useful as always. One of her "Really?" cuts of 1935, "Till the Cows Come Home," has her calling herself "a bitch from Baltimore," bragging of her sexual prowess.*** There is much in that version of *bitch*, which other early Black woman blues

---

*I likely would not know what a "betch" was if it weren't for my former Columbia student Sarah Tully putting me on to the website, for which I thank her.

**The Broadway musical version of *Legally Blonde* conveys "betchness" perhaps more perfectly (if there is a such thing as more perfect) than the movie, and I recommend a listen to the cast album, which is one of my top fifty musical scores of all time in all of its pinkness. There can be such art in what seems so, well, pink!

***Bogan requires freer quoting. Stop reading now if you'd rather—really, do not read on if you aren't ready for a jump—but this song includes the likes of "If you suck my pussy, baby, I'll suck your dick / I'll do it to you, honey, till I make you shit." One must know of such things to make it clear that freely expressed profanity did not begin in, as Philip Larkin would imply, 1963. It was just underground.

singers such as Ma Rainey are reported to have used when microphones weren't present. Black women have often remarked that they felt empowered within their own cultural context, thank you very much, long before Betty Friedan.

Their usage of *bitch* anticipates its appropriation as a term of pride by white women decades after Bogan recorded these lyrics, which surely sprang from how ordinary and unrecorded Black women used it in daily speech, applauding when they heard it sung out by performers like Rainey and Bogan.

Language change involves layers upon layers. Since the 1970s, white gay men have incorporated a degree of Black female slang into their own in-group conversation, likely stemming from a sense of shared oppression from mainstream society (some Black women have criticized this as cultural appropriation). This has included the affectionate usage of *bitch*, as in "Bitch, that color doesn't work for you," or "Bitch, you need to stop." It works as a leveler in the same way as *nigger* does among Black men. One may assume that *faggot* would be the term of choice, but that word is not as often used as an appellation, as opposed to term of reference, among gay men. "It was a room full of fags," said affectionately, is reference; "Faggot, you need to stop" is appellation. It doesn't quite land in the way that "Nigga, you need to stop" would. Rather, proper usage is that *bitch* goes in that slot.

Not only gay men have used *bitch* as a term of affection. As early as 1749, in *Tom Jones* the Squire says that "Landlord is a vast comical Bitch, you will like 'un hugely." That "'un" for him is, for the record, normal dialectal English of southwest England, and conveyed a vernacular tone, à la "You're gonna like the mothafucka." Or "You're gonna like the *son of a bitch*," an epithet that has also been used in affection as much as in disrespect, to an extent that elbows out the solo *bitch*. And not just last week or even last century on *Seinfeld*. A 1697 source includes praise of a workingman: " 'Tis a good lusty fore-handed well-set Son of a Bitch." In a direct lineage, a 2020 episode of the animated series *Bob's Burgers* had shabbily precocious tween Gene embracing his father with "Come here, you son of a bitch!"

Grammar turns up in the strangest places, and so often in profanity, as we have seen. Did you ever notice that when *son of a bitch* is used as a slur, the accent is on the *bitch*, but that when it is used in joy, the accent can be on the *son*? *Son of a bitch, that was my lucky day!* Here, too, the original meaning is obscured, and beyond the degree in "sum-bitch" where *bitch* remains vibrant. In *son of a bitch*, rendered as what we might transcribe as "sunova-bich," not only is *bitch* no longer perceptible as a word or element, but we do not hear *son* as referring to a child, given that there is no mother evident in the expression.

We have in essence a new word entirely, just as *cup* and *board* have joined into a single, indivisible word *cubberd* unconnected to cups or boards in our minds until we learn to spell. It would be even harder to trace the history of this pronunciation than of "sum-bitch," given that accent is not conventionally indicated in writing. Happily, though, sometimes it is—such as in the smutty little underground comic books I referred to regarding *fuck*. I should leave out the details, but one entry has a gentleman exclaim in delight of anticipation, "*SON* OF A BITCH!" The episode is undated, but was almost certainly drawn in the 1960s, and thus dates that pronunciation at least that far back.*

It Will Become a Pronoun.

The profanity-to-pronoun pathway, so well-trodden in twentieth-century American English, means that the surprise would be if *bitch* had not become a pronoun somewhere along the line. It has.

I mentioned that where *nigga* becomes a pronoun, it isn't used for women, and left our grid of real-life American English pronouns blank for the *she* ones of "Black Dismissive" category:

NEUTRAL	DISMISSIVE	BLACK REFLEXIVE	INTIMATE DISMISSIVE	REFLEXIVE
I / me	my ass	a nigga	myself	my shit
you	your ass		yourself	your shit

---

*Answers to the questions: (a) My father had them tucked away when I was a teenager and I made sure to "inherit" them; (b) *Archie*'s Betty and Veronica, and the utterer was Mr. Lodge! And I really will leave it there, but television's *Riverdale* pales in comparison.

NEUTRAL	DISMISSIVE	BLACK REFLEXIVE	INTIMATE DISMISSIVE	REFLEXIVE
he / him	his ass	(the) nigga	himself	his shit
she / her	her ass		herself	her shit
it	that shit	(the) nigga	itself	
we / us	our asses		ourselves	our shit
y'all	your asses		yourselves	your shit
they / them	their asses	(the) niggaz	themselves	their shit

But that was technically a bit coy. As a speech variety used by human beings in all of their gloomy imperfection, Black English does not mysteriously skip women in its pronominal creativity. An honest take on the matter is that where *nigga* can be used as a kind of third-person pronoun for men and even mosquitoes, *bitch* is used the way *nigga* is in that "slot," right down to requiring an additional *the* when used as an object. If I may, imagine *I told the bitch and she didn't listen*, pronounced as *I told the bitch and she didn't listen*. Taking the liberty of adding the plural usage as well, we now have:

NEUTRAL	DISMISSIVE	BLACK REFLEXIVE	INTIMATE DISMISSIVE	REFLEXIVE
I / me	my ass	a nigga	myself	my shit
you	your ass		yourself	your shit
he / him	his ass	(the) nigga	himself	his shit
she / her	her ass	**(the) bitch**	herself	her shit
it	that shit	(the) nigga	itself	

NEUTRAL	DISMISSIVE	BLACK REFLEXIVE	INTIMATE DISMISSIVE	REFLEXIVE
we / us	our asses		ourselves	our shit
y'all	your asses		yourselves	your shit
they / them	their asses	(the) niggaz	themselves	their shit
		(the) bitches		

In 1990, when Black Washington, DC, mayor Marion Barry was caught using crack with a woman, he yelled, "Bitch set me up!" Here, he was saying, "*She* set me up!" only with what we might term Black American inflection. Pronouns can start as real words; they aren't always blank grunts like Romance languages' *tu* for "you," which for all we know started as the spluttery squawk of toddlers somewhere around the Caspian Sea.

Spanish's *usted*, the polite pronoun for "you," started as *vuestra merced*—"your mercy"—said quickly for centuries. In languages of Vietnam and Cambodia called Chamic, a polite word for *I* started as "slave," which parallels in humility the *a nigga* usage in Black English (perhaps infelicitously), while one word for *we* is also the word for *body*. As such, there is no reason that *bitch* could not become a pronoun in the same way as *slave*, *body*, or, let's face it, *ass*, *shit*, or *nigger*.

It goes further, with Black English's *a nigga*, while we're on that subject, as a springboard. In Black English, *a bitch* can be used in the same way as *a nigga*, as a first-person pronoun for women, of all things. When pop singer Cardi B exclaimed on

Instagram, "I ain't gonna front. A bitch is scared," she was referring to herself, not a different woman. This makes the pronoun spread tidier: If there is a gender distinction in the third person, why not in the first?

We must be clear, though, that this makes the Black English pronouns more elaborate than the standard ones. Languages that have a gender distinction in the third person, as in our own *he* and *she*, are common. Ones that have a gender distinction in the first person are much less so. The example possibly known to some readers would be Japanese, with the male *ore* and the female *atashi*. But other examples tend to be more obscure and there are only so many of them. Black English brings English into that exclusive club.

After her "I ain't gonna front. A bitch is scared," Cardi B appended, "Shit got me panicking"—here were vernacular American English pronouns in action. Our full chart, then, is this:

NEUTRAL	DISMISSIVE	BLACK REFLEXIVE	INTIMATE DISMISSIVE	REFLEXIVE
I / me	my ass	a nigga / **a bitch**	myself	my shit
you	your ass		yourself	your shit
he / him	his ass	(the) nigga	himself	his shit
she / her	her ass	(the) bitch	herself	her shit
it	that shit	(the) nigga	itself	
we / us	our asses		ourselves	our shit

NEUTRAL	DISMISSIVE	BLACK REFLEXIVE	INTIMATE DISMISSIVE	REFLEXIVE
y'all	your asses		yourselves	your shit
they / them	their asses	(the) niggaz	themselves	their shit
		(the) bitches		

It Will Become Grammar in Other Ways That Strain Belief.

No medieval could ever have imagined that we would use *ass* in expressions like *big-ass pot*, or *fuck* in expressions like *he didn't do fuck-all*. Recall also how *hell* in a phrase like *the hell I will* is in a disembodied state, with a meaning that corresponds in no recoverable way at all with its original one.

In this vein, one of *bitch*'s renditions is so abstract as to put us somewhere between late Beethoven string quartets and John Cage: *flip a bitch*, which refers to making an illegal U-turn. I heard it used once in 1998 in the Bay Area of California by some sparklingly witty gals I was in a car with. I have brought it up to the bafflement of many East Coast colleagues since, but Urban Dictionary assures me that the expression was by no means a quirk of those pals of mine. Yet how *bitch* makes sense there is an open question. Almost certainly it includes the idea that this illegal move qualifies, in its insubordination, as "bitchy." The *flip* may start from flipping someone a bird, although that expression is a little elderly to have served as the source of a phrase that seems to have emerged near the end of the twentieth century. Whatever they were, the steps involved in likening a nervy move when driving to a female person who doesn't take any guff leave one in a certain awe. A word Iron Age Europeans used to refer to female dogs is now used *on the other side of the other side* of the world in California to refer to making illegal U-turns.

And just as confoundingly, *bitch* can connote, as a word with some pepper, extremity. *Hot as hell, hot as shit, hot-ass day*—this happens, and thus with *son of a bitch*, we get William Burroughs in *Junkie* saying in 1953, "I hit Philly sick as a son-ofabitch." Or Clark Gable saying, "I worked like a son of a bitch to learn a few tricks." Nor was this a modernish Americanism: way back in 1828, someone else, the son of a British slaveowner in Barbados "worked like a son of a bitch" in place of a slave about to be whipped.

Note how meaning here has slipped the bounds of form: one works in a fashion akin to someone birthed by a female dog? Why do we assume that the puppy works hard, or does anything in a fashion other than the idle, random sort that puppies are given to? If in Philadelphia you are as sick as a son of a bitch, does that mean that you are sick in a fashion associated with some specific way that one gets sick if one happens to be an asshole?

Clearly not—connection with dictionary meaning is long lost; *son of a bitch* here simply means "to a great degree." An opprobrious term for women, or progeny of women, now means just "extremely." That is, *truly*, *actually*, and *really* have been joined by a word originally used to refer to dogs that are female. Go figure.

———————

With such a wide array of uses over such a vast period of time, *bitch* may not seem profane in the sense of the first six of our nine words, or even of *nigger*. However, its fertility just means that it exists in many versions. We process *shit* as a "bad word" despite it having penetrated every mundane corner of how we express ourselves. In the same way, for all of the *life's a bitch* and *something else to bitch about* and *How about that, bitchez?*, imagine your nine-year-old experiencing friction with a girl in school and referring to her as a *bitch* while chomping on her peanut butter and jelly sandwich.

The horror you sense—which would only abate if the girl were about seventeen or older—is evidence that the original epithet maintains its power. Lucille Bogan may have proudly called herself a *bitch* of a certain kind in song in 1935, but in *The Color Purple*, with its mise-en-scène in which a singer like Bogan and her music would have been very much in place, there's a reason that what drives Sofia to tear a woman up is when the little lady dares to call her that. It's a fightin' word—the ninth of our lexical taboos.

* 9 *

A MOTHERFUCKING
ADDENDUM

There is one profane word we have not gotten to, partly because it would have made the chapter on *fuck* too long and partly because it will serve well as a bit of after-dinner brandy. I refer to none other than grand old *motherfucker*, which despite its ordinariness to us would be especially fun to try to explain to a newcomer to the language.

I will never forget a clerical job I had in the summer of 1987 in Philadelphia. It was in an open office with a vast field of desks à la *The Apartment*—no cubicles. A good fifty people could see and hear one another all day long, and one person it was hard to miss was Pat.

Roughly, if *Sanford and Son*'s Aunt Esther were the oldest sister and *The Jeffersons*' Florence were the youngest, Pat was the middle one, likely fifty and a bit, and prominently irreverent, loudish, the office cut-up—imagine Tyler Perry's Madea preretirement. Frank, meanwhile, was a white guy who worked in a department upstairs that had some administrative relationship with our floor that I wasn't there long enough to really understand, which occasioned him to come down two or three times a day. Physically and in terms of personality, he was the love child of Mr. Roper from *Three's Company* and the Pillsbury Doughboy, about fifty like Pat.

The two had jobs of similar level in the company's hierarchy. They had a running joke where Frank would hint at a sense of status higher than his actual "station" in the organization and Pat would feign indignation and rake him over the coals. Once, for example, Frank had apparently directed someone in another department to send a memo to him addressing him as "Mister [his last name]" instead of "Frank," with Pat sensing this as implying that he was a bigger wheel than he was.

Her haranguing him was always full of half-finished sentences and pregnant intonations just shy of calling him assorted names inappropriate in an office setting, which would have everybody chuckling already. "You little…" she would start to say. "Keep that up and they're gonna…" with her intonation alone signaling, without her enunciating it, a subsequent "kick you out on your little [white] ass." After he left, having wanly defended himself, Pat would go back to her desk and keep chastely assailing him under her breath so that everybody could hear it. After about a half minute, first looking to make sure the boss wasn't at her desk at the head of the pool (which she usually wasn't), Pat would sound off with "MothaFUCKuh!," grinding her teeth into her lip on the *f* with a good, smoky hiss.

Which was what she had been all but saying for the past five minutes, flirting with it like a moth around a flame. Her finally nailing the actual word was a catharsis, technically a payoff, but it felt almost like, yes, a climax, and the office—about half Black women—would burst out into raucous guffaws that lasted a good minute. They would die down after thirty seconds, but then somebody would start cackling again (once it was me!) and everybody would take back up with them. I wonder whether the (white, likely South Philly Italian) boss lady ever caught on to these outbursts, and whether Frank ever actually heard Pat calling him the name.

That "Mother*fucker*!" was possibly the funniest thing I have ever heard in my life, and partly because there was something larger in the scenario, after all—the Black lady taking the white man down a peg publicly, which would have been socially un-likely as little as about fifteen years before 1987. It wouldn't have been as funny if Frank were Black, or even if he hadn't been a rather small, gentle man who clearly did not merit being tarred in such a way (how much of a motherfucker could the Pillsbury Doughboy be?). Or, if it hadn't all been in fun. Pat always made it clear when Frank was in the room that all of this was just a routine, often throwing her arms around him and saying how much she loved him.

But above all, it wouldn't have been funny if Pat weren't

Black. Note that the whole thing fails to translate with a white Pat of any kind. For example, taking funny white television actresses of a certain age and vernacular affect at the time, the "script" wouldn't have made any sense with Selma Diamond, Doris Roberts, or even Polly Holliday as her country-gal Flo character on *Alice*. This is symptomatic of the fact that while there's something about *fuck*, there's something Black about *motherfucker*.

It's Kanye West who pops off with it while visiting the Oval Office, whereas it's harder to imagine even as out of control a white fellow as Justin Bieber doing that. It's Louis Armstrong who referred to Arkansas governor Orville Faubus as a "no-good motherfucker" (toned down in the press to "ignorant ploughboy"); it would have been less likely of, say, Buddy Hackett despite his potty mouth in unrecorded contexts. It's Louis Armstrong's wife who, after a bit of whiskey, was given to some use of the word; Bing Crosby's wife Dixie Lee, one safely assumes, used it less, despite that she drank much more! It was Redd Foxx's record company that was called MF, not Rodney Dangerfield's.

It settled in as a single curse word later than one might suppose. There are no medieval records of someone calling an enemy a "palsied mutherfokere" or the like. To be sure, recreational slander referring to the sexual habits of people's mothers is common worldwide and has a rich history in English. In 1831, famed conjoined twins Chang and Eng Bunker were physically assaulted by a man who, the twins were quoted as saying, "Call me and my mother hard name." The name may have been *motherfucker*, but it muddies matters that a reporter described the offense as "using opprobrious epithets in relation to their mother," which may have meant speculating as to the sexual habits of their mother apart from activities with her sons. The specific term *motherfucker* only appears explicitly in the later nineteenth century, first intended in its literal meaning, but gradually becoming a near-nonsense eruption.

The word did not emerge with this Black flavor. The earliest usage as yet known is in 1890, when the Texas Court of Appeals reports someone saying in 1889 "that God damned motherf—king, bastardly son-of-a-bitch!" Then in 1897, a man asked to be charged with manslaughter rather than murder because of having been called a "mother-fucking son-of-a-bitch." He was turned down, but his request suggests the term packed a kind of wallop, implying that it was then either new or newish. These reports do not specify the miscreants' race, but presumably if the men were "colored," in as implacably bigoted and segregated an era as the 1890s, it would have been noted.

Just why *motherfucker* came to be especially embraced by Black people is a mystery. Athletic speculations as to perspectives and sensitivities on motherhood and intercourse unique to Black Americans are unlikely to yield much, and the most plausible explanation is likely the dullest—chance. Just as one can't know "why" Brits say *would have done* where Americans say *would have*, the term *motherfucker* likely just happened to catch on among Black people in the same way that hacky sack caught on among white ones. If we rolled the tape again, possibly Black guys would be standing in circles kicking little sandbags around and the Rat Pack would have been calling one another motherfuckers.

But instead, it was indeed among Black men that the word was liberally used in the "toast" literature of the twentieth century, as in the classic "Signifyin' Monkey" couplet "Said the signifying monkey to the lion that very same day / There's a bad motherfucker heading your way." The use of this word in this body of work, in fact, is valuable and vibrant evidence of *fuck* before the 1960s. In no sense can we say there is no "real" attestation of it just because professors weren't including it on the printed pages of dictionaries.

However, if there is room for considering artificial and yet totemic milestones in cases like this, the word was officially stamped in the American consciousness as a Black, or at least Blackish, term, with Amiri Baraka's poem "Black People" in 1968:

All the stores will open if you say the magic words. The
magic words are: Up against the wall mother fucker this is
a stick up!... Let's get together and kill him my man.

That same year, a friend of mine, a Black woman who at the time would have been reminiscent of the nurse character Julia that Diahann Carroll played on television in her reserved and middle-class demeanor, attended a party. There, two Black men genially teased her for not being able to say *motherfucker* in what they regarded as the properly "Black" way. Don King shared these guys' sense of ownership of the word, arguing four years later:

> *We're blacks and we have nothing. We don't have expensive suits, or big houses, or luxury vacations. We're poor. All we got is the word. Our only invention that belongs to us is a word. And that word is* motherfucker! *Nobody can take that away from us. That's our word. That's a black word. We should be proud of that word. It's our heritage.*

King then successfully got a dignified elderly Black couple, churchgoing folk, to shout out "Motherfucker!" in salute—it was a new era for an old word. I also recall a Black camp counselor I had in 1980 who was fond of the term but euphemized it for us kiddies as "Martin farmer." The white counselors had other terms (and didn't euphemize them much!). In the 2008 musical *[title of show]*, at an especially goofy moment one of the white male actors personifies an idea of his as an anthropomorphic character singing a song, à la the "bill" character going through Congress in the *Schoolhouse Rock!* cartoon segment. The character genially calls another character "muthafucka," the idea being that the idea is, for some reason, supposed to be of Black ethnicity (it's an odd show).

The word wouldn't be card-carrying English profanity if it made any sense, and *motherfucker* has drifted long past that. It no longer refers to anything maternal. Surely sex was the origin of the term, given how common insults about mothers and sex are worldwide. However, in our times, is anyone thinking about incest when tossing off that word, especially when among Black men the word often simply means "fella" or, in the plural, "ordinary folks"? "Ten million motherfuckers freebasing, and I'm the one who blows up!" Richard Pryor said—what did that have to do with the sexual habits of the motherfuckers in question? And when it's about inanimate objects, we really aren't in Kansas anymore:

> *It seemed fair to kill my car to me, right, 'cause my wife was going to leave my ass. I say "Not in this motherfucker you ain't. Uh-uh. If you leave me you be drivin' them Hush Puppies you got on. 'Cause I'm gonna kill this motherfucker here."*

The *mother* in *motherfucker* is now less a bit of meaning than an opaque splotch, almost as unrelated to its original meaning as the *French* in *French fries*, where calls during the George W. Bush administration to call them "Freedom fries," in protest against France's opposition to America's invasion of Iraq, seemed so absurd because no one thinks of the name of the food as having anything to do with France. Especially when *motherfucker* is spoken rapidly, and even elided in rapid speech to "muh-fucka," we lose all reference to parentage just as in *cupboard* we hardly think of cups.

Here, *mother* is but a piquant, rhythmical windup to the *fucker*, practically a prefix, and a meaningless one. We get a sense of how the word would feel if we really were thinking about mothers from a man I once knew recently arrived from the Czech Republic who, offended by the behavior of a certain unseemly individual, ran after him yelling, "Fuckamotha! Fuckamotha!" He was in there pitching—the individual in question was indeed quite the motherfucker—but our infuriated Czech had the order wrong. Why I could barely help laughing on the spot is that "fuckamotha" makes us think about the action in question. One wanted to say to the guy "It's not really about fucking a mother!" Because it isn't.

It is, of all things, less Czech than Southeast Asian. In some languages, you can add a bit of punch to a word by simply adding an extra piece that doesn't mean anything by itself. In Cambodian, to decay is *daap*. But another way to say decay is *don-daap*, kind of like you can say *jabber* but also *jibber-jabber*. The *don-* is, itself, meaningless; a Cambodian will often shrug when asked what the difference is between *daap*ing and *don-dapp*ing. To tell someone they speak well you tell them they *prac*; to level the compliment with a bit more dash or color is to render it as *prohk-prac*. *Prohk*, alone, is just a meaningless clump.

In the grand scheme of things, whatever people meant by *motherfucker* in nineteenth-century Texas, these days the *mother* part is essentially akin to *jibber-*, *don-*, and *prohk-*. *Mother* has the same first vowel sound (although not vowel *letter*) and the same rhythm as *fucker* and thus happens to match it nicely, as *jibber* does *jabber*. Hence *motherfucker* has become, in the grand scheme of things (to the extent that this instance lends itself to an analysis as grand), simply the way we usually say *fucker*.

Note that *fucker* by itself is less common. When we imagine someone calling a person "Fucker!" we almost feel like it should be politely corrected to the more idiomatic "*Mother*fucker." In a way, this is grammatical irregularity—to render *fuck* as a noun we not only tack *-er* to the end but also hang on to the front end, of all things, *mother*.

For a spell Broadway was graced with a play called *The Motherfucker with the Hat*—*motherfucker* is *fucker* with a hat on. There is complexity in profanity, then, even of the humblest variety. *Jibber-jabber, tittle-tattle, pitter-patter, mother-fucker.*

ACKNOWLEDGMENTS

Endless thanks to my agent, Dan Conaway, for contributing the very idea of this book and shepherding it into reality with such expertise and sheer savvy. I have also been dazzled by the production team at Penguin Random House in turning some thousands of words into a saleable item. Also, along the way Robert LoBiondo and Joe Zellnik gave me handy examples—respectively, what you learn in this book about language on *The Jeffersons* and a certain usage of the word *bitch* I owe to them.

NOTES

Where unattributed, most of the earlier uses of our nasty words in this book are drawn from the *Oxford English Dictionary*, with my contribution being to explain and illuminate their significance. Basic and uncontroversial facts about the history of our words, available in countless venues, are not sourced here, nor are news stories. The internet allows a reconception of the purpose of reference sections like this. I here provide sources for the more idiosyncratic references in the text, although even some of these are trackable online.

Introduction

Affadavit from Babe Ruth's father: Jane Leavy, *The Big Fella: Babe Ruth and the World He Created* (New York: Harper, 2018), 49.
Bella Abzug: I have this from senior newsmen who were in a position to know.

Chapter 1: *Damn* and *Hell*: English's First Bad Words

In general, I found Ashley Montagu, *The Anatomy of Swearing* (New York: Macmillan, 1967) especially useful for this chapter.
Hobo recollection: Mimi, "Meet Virginia Stopher, 19-year-old Girl Hobo of the 1920s Who Left Her Husband to Ride the Rails," *Slate*, January 26, 2019.

Frank Lloyd Wright: Paul Hendrickson, *Plagued by Fire: The Dreams and Furies of Frank Lloyd Wright* (New York: Knopf, 2019), 169.

Art Young: Nancy Milford, *Savage Beauty: The Life of Edna St. Vincent Millay* (New York: Random House, 2002), 162.

Oh my God's trajectory: Sali Tagliamonte and Bridget L. Jankowski, Golly, gosh, and Oh, my God!: What North American dialects can tell us about swear words, *American Speech*, no. 94 (2019): 195–222.

Chapter 2: What Is It About *Fuck*?

Anatoly Liberman's exhaustive coverage of *fuck*'s family tree in his magisterial *An Analytic Dictionary of English Etymology: An Introduction* (Minneapolis: University of Minnesota Press, 2008) is useful on the prehistory of the word. I differ with him on a point or two, but one must start there nevertheless, and data in this chapter on Germanic precursors and cousins of the word come mostly from Liberman.

Maxwell Perkins: A. Scott Berg, *Max Perkins: Editor of Genius* (New York: Penguin, 1978), 5.

WWI soldiers: John Brophy and Eric Partridge, eds., *Songs and Slang of the British Soldier, 1914–1918* (E. Partridge Ltd., 1930).

Shamus Culhane: Leonard Maltin, *Of Mice and Magic: A History of American Animated Cartoons* (New York: Plume, 1981), 248.

Dorothy Parker: Kevin C. Fitzpatrick, ed., *Dorothy Parker: Complete Broadway, 1918–1923* (iUniverse, 2014), 288.

Jackie Gleason in *Follow the Girls*: Ethan Mordden, *Better Foot Forward* (Grossmann, 1976), 203–5.

Elaine Stritch: the documentary *Elaine Stritch: Shoot Me* (2013).

Chapter 3: Profanity and Shit

Jesse Sheidlower's *The F-Word* (Oxford University Press, 2009) will forever be the go-to source for those interested in *fuck* in all of its manifestations.

St. Vincent Millay and her sister cussing: Nancy Milford, *Savage Beauty*, 163.

Allen Walker Read latrine book: Allen Walker Read, *Lexical Evidence from Folk Epigraphy in Western North America* (self-published, 1935).

Laurel and Hardy film: *A Perfect Day* (1929).

Chapter 4: A Kick-*Ass* Little Word

Geoff Nunberg wrote the authoritative text on *asshole*, *The Ascent of the A-Word: Assholism, the First Sixty Years* in 2012. I recommend it, in observance of the passing as this book was in production of one of my closest friend-colleagues in linguistics, as a lesson in how to process language as a living, quirky, and analytical person.

Tarkington: Robert Gottlieb, "The Rise and Fall of Booth Tarkington," *The New Yorker*, November 11, 2019.

Follow the Girls: Ethan Mordden, *Better Foot Forward* (Grossmann, 1976), 203–5.

Stuntman for John Ford: Scott Eyman, *Print the Legend: The Life and Times of John Ford* (New York: Simon & Schuster, 2015), 140.

Chapter 5: Those Certain Parts

Russian expressions: Edward Topol, Dermo! *The Real Russian Tolstoy Never Used* (New York: Plume, 1997).

St. Vincent Millay and "kitty": Nancy Milford, *Savage Beauty*, 356.

Chapter 6: Why Do We Call It "The N-Word"?

Herskovits: Charles King, *Gods of the Upper Air* (New York: Anchor, 2019), 61.

Ex-slave interviews: They can be read on this invaluable Library of Congress website:

https://www.loc.gov/collections/slave-narratives-from-the-federal-writers -project-1936-to-1938/about-this-collection/

Cat in the toilet: Taylor Jones and Christopher Hall, "Grammatical analysis and the multiple N-words in African American English," *American Speech*, no. 94: 478–512.

A nigga pronoun: see above.

Chapter 7: The Other F-Word

Faggot for *child*: Chris Bourne, "The Surprisingly Complex History of Brits Saying 'Bum a Fag,'" *MEL Magazine*, April 17, 2019.

Paresis Hall scene: Luc Sante, *Low Life* (New York: Macmillan, 2003), 397.

1911 exchange: Dale Cockrell, *Everybody's Doin' It: Sex, Music, and Dance in New York: 1840–1917* (New York: W.W. Norton, 2019), 220.

Chapter 8: Being in Total Control, Honey!

Gay Divorce drum smack: Robert Kimball, ed., *The Complete Lyrics of Cole Porter* (New York: Knopf, 1987), 109.

Chapter 9: A Motherfucking Addendum

One can learn all there is to know about *motherfucker* from Jim Dawson's *The Compleat Motherfucker: A History of the Mother of All Dirty Words* (Port Townsend, WA: Feral, 2009). It supplied many of the examples in this chapter. The sheer generosity of the book may wear you to a nub after awhile, but we must be thankful for its existence partly as just an invaluable reference source.

Chang and Eng: Yunte Huang, *Inseparable: The Original Siamese Twins and Their Rendezvous with American History* (New York: Liveright, 2018), 115.

Also by
John McWhorter